The Common Ventur[e] of Life

The Common Ventures of Life

MARRIAGE, BIRTH, WORK AND DEATH

BY

Elton Trueblood

WORD BOOKS, PUBLISHER

Waco, Texas

THE COMMON VENTURES OF LIFE

Printed in the United States of America

First Word quality paperback edition published in April 1975.

To PAULINE *and* MARTIN

and MARGARET *and* ARNOLD

and SAMUEL *and* ELIZABETH

whose names appear with mine

on the pages between the testaments

of our family Bible

Contents

Preface

THE purpose of this book is to help puzzled men and women to prepare for the intelligent and reverent facing of those experiences which are so central to man's life that they have seemed supreme in all generations and in all cultures. There are a few points at which the primary stuff of reality comes so close to the surface that even the least sensitive of men are forced into awareness. These come to pagans and to Christians alike as they come both to the prepared and to the unprepared. As we analyze such experiences we find that there are four which stand in a class alone, markedly different from all others in human importance. In spite of all changes in the externals of man's life, these go on, though they do not always go on well. If the race continues, men will continue to fall in love, to produce children, to work with hand and brain, and to die.

Each of these experiences is fundamentally a venture. Each primary human step is a leap in the sense that it reaches into the unknown, though it is never a wild leap. The necessary faith is, in each instance, a reasonable faith. Whatever happens to our religion, and whatever happens to our governments, as long as there are people at all we shall go on falling in love and bearing children and finding work to do and dying. *The best life for mankind will always be that life in which the inevitable experiences are undertaken with the most intelligence, reverence and courage.*

Though contemporary man necessarily shares in these fundamental ventures, as all our fathers have done, we now do so with a serious handicap. *We are culturally uprooted.* We have received such a shock in our time that we do not know how to live. We are fairly clear about money and we have some definite ideas about government, but about the major issues of life and death we have almost no ideas at all. The true seriousness of our situation is hidden from us by virtue of the relative stability of the material aspects of our culture, but it stands revealed when the characteristic man of our time faces those human crises which have long constituted the supreme moments of our common life. Many are pathetically bewildered because the religious frame in which these universal experiences have long been set has been so nearly shattered. They flounder helplessly and alone. The experiences which might reveal so much of the glory and pathos of human life become dull prose. What might mean so much consequently means so little.

My hope is that these pages will be read, not primarily by the already devout, but by some of the millions who are literally between two worlds, one dead and the other powerless to be born. I hope that some of the many who are wholly outside the organized Church will read this little book and find some guidance in the facing of their own inevitable problems. Since such is the purpose of the book, it includes not only the four chapters on the four fundamental ventures which are of crucial importance in the structure of common life, but also an introductory chapter which outlines the philosophy of wholeness which underlies the entire conception. The major premise of this philosophy is the conviction that ours is a sacramental universe.

As it now stands, the book comprises the first set of Willson Lectures given in 1948 at Southwestern University, Georgetown, Texas. I am glad to be able to take advantage of the opportunity to express my gratitude to President J. N. R. Score for his great kindness in helping to make the book possible.

E.T.

Earlham College
October 1, 1948

The Common Ventures of Life

CHAPTER I

The Recovery of Wholeness

It is using a pick-axe to no purpose that makes a prison.

ANTOINE DE SAINT-EXUPÉRY

CHRISTIANITY is the most avowedly materialistic of the great world religions. There are religions which are almost purely "spiritual" in their outlook, largely ignoring the body and the whole material order, but the Christian faith is not one of them. According to the Gospel, the true function of spirit is not to deny matter, but rather to glorify it. The Word, we believe, was made *flesh*. The Bible is a highly materialist book beginning with the assertion that man was made from dust, and concerned at all points with what happens to bodies, especially broken and needy bodies. The Gospel records the feeding of the hungry and the healing of the sick. Christian teaching centers, not on a realm of pure supersensual Being, but rather on the divine revelation through a mundane historical process, in particular times and in particular places.

Christianity is committed to belief in the ultimate significance of this historical process rather than to a set of ideas independent of events.

It is only when we begin to realize the contrast between Christianity and all forms of spiritualism that we understand the reason for many characteristic features of Christian experience. Only a religion concerned with the flesh as well as with the spirit would found hospitals; only a religion so concerned would turn naturally to feeding the hungry and to the provision of medical supplies. Medical science is frankly physical, *materia medica* we call it, yet it is largely through the missionary enterprise that medical schools have been introduced into many parts of our world. Because, in its best expressions, the Christian Church has recognized that people need milk as well as preaching, the Brethren have sent heifers to Europe and Christian missionaries have established dairies in India. It has been a great part of the genius of the Christian religion to recognize that men are not angels and to refuse to treat them as if they *were* angels. Angels, if they exist, are pure spirits without bodily needs, but men are not pure spirits. Men are combinations of body and mind and spirit, uniting in a working partnership both hand and brain. They thus have a variety of temptations and any valid religion will be frankly concerned with all of these.

Though the recognition of the wholeness of man both in his material and in his spiritual aspects has been the major tradition in the West for many centuries, pressure is exerted from two sides with the aim of separating as widely as possible the realms of matter and of spirit. The pressure from one side is that of modern natural science, with its program of explanation of all phenomena by reference to physical categories. The ideal of all the sciences, best exemplified in physics, is that of accounting for all events by efficient causation as against purpose or determination by recognition of the good. There is no doubt that this program has been, on the whole, a beneficent one, since it has done so much to eliminate superstition. If a disease can be accounted for by reference to a germ, it is a good thing not to confuse the situation by reference to demons or to other purposive agents. Methodologically this tendency in science has been nothing more than a particular application of the principle of parsimony; *there is no point in having two explanations of an event when one will suffice.*

Grateful as we may be for this scientific emphasis on efficient as against final causation, great distortion ensues when what is primarily a method becomes a dogma. It is easy for us to slip over to the gratuitous affirmation that anything which does not follow the laws of matter has no real existence. Such a position is not demanded by modern science and is explicitly discouraged by many distinguished scientific thinkers, but there is no doubt that this position is the heart of the philosophy of many for whom science has come to be almost a religion. Sometimes this dogma is overtly championed, but it appears more often as an unconscious or unstated premise. For such persons, spirit is bound to seem an alien factor in this essentially material world and a mere result of material causes rather than an effective cause making a radical difference in the course of events. This is to destroy the wholeness of man by a virtual denial of spirit. It is not required by science and it is not good philosophy.

The other common way in which the wholeness of man is denied, and our major tradition thus neglected, is the religious way. In many religious movements there is a constant pressure to keep the spiritual life free from contamination with the material, which is looked upon as gross and crass. The ideal of some devoted persons is to set the spirit free from the body and its embarrassing demands. Thus celibacy is looked upon as a higher ideal than marriage while contemplation and prayer are counted more noble than work with the hands. Meditation is seen as more truly religious than is the work of the doctor who finds the material cause of a dread disease and eliminates it.

It is an easy step from this antimaterialist religion to that which fears what it considers a too great concern for mundane affairs. Thus we find many who cry out against "political preaching," holding that the Church must tend to its own business, which is the saving of souls. Churches which try to make their influence felt in the promotion of legislation or in the removal of racial discrimination or in the raising of wages are criticized severely for departure from their true and major function. Helping men to have better wages, so that their families can live in decent houses and avoid the diseases which come from exposure and filth, is not, some say, a religious task at all; it is grossly secular and should be left to secular agencies.

These two divisive movements, one from the side of science and the other from the side of religion, have the same effect. Both serve to break the unity of life and the result, as ought to be expected, is uniformly bad. The purpose of spirit is to *control* matter and the purpose of matter is to *serve* spirit, but when the two are severed, this beneficent relationship is impossible. If scientific materialism is accepted as true, the nerve of creative effort is cut, for what is the use of bringing creative purpose to bear on situations where the only causes which are effective are purely material ones? The theoretical materialist himself, if he is intellectually consistent, will hold that his own acts are conditioned in wholly material ways and that his decision to seek truth or to relieve pain has no bearing on the issue whatsoever. On the other hand, if the religion of pure spirit is accepted as true, the nerve of effort is likewise cut. Why try to improve material conditions if they have no real significance? Why try to cure disease or overcome poverty if the good life is wholly independent of these? Why try to remove physical evils if religion transcends them? The concrete result is to let the physical or the temporal go its own way unchecked by spirit. "The material world, with all man's economic activity, becomes a happy hunting-ground for uncurbed acquisitiveness, and religion becomes a refined occupation for the leisure of the mystical."[1]

Since this book is not primarily about science, but primarily about religion, our chief interest, in these pages, lies in the ways in which current religion fails to keep the unity of human life and, more especially, in the ways in which this unity may be restored. It is unfortunately clear that a great deal of our current religion, including the Christian religion, touches the life of ordinary men and women at distressingly few points. Most people, when they discuss what religion means, make reference to only one

[1] William Temple, *Nature, Man and God* (London: The Macmillan Company, 1934), p. 486. The whole of chap. XIX is highly relevant.

activity—church-going. Now there is no doubt about the importance of church-going, inasmuch as men and women are fallible creatures who need desperately the reminders which church-going provides, but a religion which stops with this is wretchedly weak, too weak to revive our sagging culture. Christianity lives or dies, not by what goes on in the churches, but by what goes on outside them.

The one hour a week in church is relatively ineffective because it seems to people to be remote from the rest of living, and consequently irrelevant. Most of the time we are working, sleeping, governing, playing, begetting children, growing, suffering. What goes on in church seems to many to belong to some other world, with its antique language and its particular emotions, suitable only for such separated occasions. The hour of worship seems to demonstrate the epiphenomenalism implicit in so much physical science; it goes along with our ordinary life at one point, but it is not causally effective in that life any more than the rainbow is causally effective on the cloud on which it seems to ride.

If we wish to have a really important religion we must make a complete break with the one-hour-a-week concept. We must see our religion, not primarily as what goes on in a peculiar building with pointed arches and stained-glass windows, but as the *way* in which all ordinary enterprises are conducted. It must be connected with the way we *eat*, the way we *work*, the way we *make love*, the way we *think*, the way we *dream*, the way we *die*. We must become aware of the devotional paradox to the effect that frequently the books which are most conducive to the spirit of devotion were not written for that purpose and are not usually classified as relgious books at all. Religion, to be effective, must be envisaged, not as one enterprise among others, but as the frame in which *all* enterprises are set. *That religion will have most meaning which touches common life redemptively at the most points.*

The unfortunate fact is that so much of our current Christianity fails when judged by this high standard. Once religious life tended to be inclusive and pervasive, but now we have succeeded in secularizing one area after another. By secularizing we mean the process of envisaging some experience apart from the context of the will of the Living God. Most activities in the life of modern man now have no explicit references to religion at all, though once they were inspired by it. *Healing* has been turned over to the physician, *death* has been turned over, in large measure, to the mortician, *education* has been turned over to the school, and *work* has been turned over to the labor union. The indication is that the majority of modern families have given up grace before meat, so that eating is coming to be little more than a biological process. Those with disturbed minds are now usually directed to psychiatrists rather than to spiritual counselors.

What is left for religion when all these are abstracted from it? Religion itself becomes an abstraction, dealing with a soul, the existence of which seems meaningless when separated from all its normal activities. If this process goes on it means inevitable decline. That which has no real function does not long endure. This development involves eventual tragedy, not for the Church, which will somehow survive, but for the organized life of man as a whole, which cannot endure without moral and spiritual supports. It is not conceivable that life can become good or remain good if it is lived on the wholly secular level. The reason for this is that man's life requires unity whereas secularization fractures the unity. Men who do not combine in one context both the temporal and the eternal will finally lose even the temporal.

We understand better the importance, in practical experience, of the reidentification of religion and common life, if we consider carefully man's place in nature. After a century of controversy and inquiry, the problem of man's place in nature now has a relatively clear answer about which there is agreement on the part of qualified thinkers. We find that man is deeply imbedded in the historical process of creation and has links with all parts of that creation. Physically he is cousin to the higher animals. The geological records indicate a long process of development without which man, as we know him, would not be. Though there are aspects of man's experience which are qualitatively different from all others as known, he is not alien to the world which spawns him.

What we discover as we look at our world philosophically is a series of levels or stratifications of reality. The lowest level, and apparently the earliest, is mere *matter*, with its mechanical basis. Above this is *life* which, in its characteristic forms, grows and reproduces itself in one way or another. The third level is *animal mind*, which, in its characteristic forms, seeks means to the satisfaction of instinctive appetites. The fourth level, *spirit*, not merely chooses between means, as animal mind does, but proceeds to the choice between *ends*, by referring to a recognized ideal standard of good.

These levels are by no means wholly separated, but are connected in specific ways. In each case the lower is necessary to the actuality of the higher, but the higher controls and utilizes all the levels beneath it. Man includes all four levels in that he is material, living, mental and spiritual all in one. So far as we can tell, a tree includes only two of these levels. Furthermore, the true value of the lower levels becomes clear only when they are utilized by the higher. The whole series begins to look like an amazing result of divine purpose, such as we should expect to find if the hypothesis that this is God's world is really true.

Now an important point to note is the way in which this philosophy unites man with nature at the same time that it elevates him above nature by recognition of the unique *differentia* of spirit. It is a part of man's glory that he can apprehend the long process of development through geologic ages, but the more he apprehends the process the more he becomes certain that he is an integral part of that same process. *He has emerged in the midst of the process which he apprehends.* Not only does our bodily structure show physical kinship with the bodies of animals, but our mental operations show intellectual kinship with animal minds. Part of our glory is thinking, but thinking did not begin with us. It is now universally admitted that the higher animals think and even reason, in the sense that they reflect on the means which will be adequate to the achievement of certain ends, especially those relating to bodily appetites. But even this thinking of the higher animals is rooted in something more elemental, the whole process of adjustment between organism and environment. We know that, though we recognize the difference between the characteristic plant and the characteristic animal, there are untold numbers of creatures which seem to belong to intermediate stages. It is hard to decide whether they are plants or animals, and it is not important that we should be able to decide. What they teach us is the way in which the world, with all its changes, is an amazingly *continuous* process. This means that man is akin, not merely to the higher animals, but to all creatures who have ever lived.

There was a time when some people were shocked at the realization that they were so deeply imbedded in nature. This connection seemed to debase man, to make him nothing but an animal or even primordial scum. Now, however, we can be grateful for the fact that so much informed opinion has been emancipated from such fears. The only condition under which man's kinship with nature would seem debasing is that according to which we accept the dogma of reduction. The dogma of reduction holds that, when the lower develops into the higher, the higher is *nothing but* the lower in disguise. Thus, if religion has developed from primitive taboo, it is, in essence, nothing but primitive taboo, on the supposition that origins give true meanings. Very fortunately this "philosophy of nothing but" now has almost no upholders and it is seen today as the prejudice it has been all along. More mature reflection makes us realize that the goal tells us something important about the entire process. We have seen again the great wisdom in Aristotle's dictum that you see what anything *is* when you see what it is *becoming*. By this standard, the kinship of man and nature does not degrade man, but rather glorifies and elevates nature. Ours is the kind of world which, from the beginning, was preparing for the emergence of creatures who, with all their sins, would be able to appreciate values and choose by reference to the good.

The fact that spirit is, at any point, part of the continuous cosmic process is the most important single fact we know about the process. The fact that minds like ours can occur in nature tells us something most revealing about the course of nature. That the world should give rise to creatures sensitive to values and concerned with duty gives one clue to the secret of the nature of the world. Unless streams rise higher than their sources, ours has been, all along, the kind of world in which value is integral to the total situation. Ours is a world which is pregnant with life, mind and spirit, even though the gestation period has been amazingly long. In short, the more we identify our spirits with the rest of the natural order, the more we see matter and spirit as a mutually beneficent combination and the more we are compelled, in reason, to posit the reality of a transcendent Creator of both.

Deeply imbedded in the Christian world view is a conception which is consistent with the wholeness of life to which evolution bears witness. This is the conception of the *sacramental.* There have been differences, in Christian history, concerning the ways in which the sacraments should be observed, and there have been differences concerning the number of the sacraments, but insistence on the sacramental idea has been well-nigh universal. The essence of the sacramental is the way in which the spiritual and the material intertwine, making the latter the vehicle of the former. A sacrament is "an actual conveyance of spiritual meaning and power by a material process," or as Augustine said, and Calvin repeated, "a visible form of an invisible grace."

The sacramental is always a recognition of divine revelation by virtue of some utterly common substance. Baptism employs common water, that which already constitutes most of our bodies, that without which organisms cannot live, and that which appears in one form or another on every part of the earth's surface. So ubiquitous and so protean is water that the first philosopher of the Western world considered it the elemental stuff to which all else was reducible. Now it is this most democratic of liquids that has been employed for centuries to mark the entrance into the Christian community. In similar fashion bread and wine, the most common of ancient foods, have been used in Holy Communion. Bread made from ordinary wheat, growing out of the stony earth has seemed to some Christians to be, in very truth, the body of our Lord.

Though we may differ in our metaphysical interpretation of these acts and though, for some of us, the concentration on a *few* such sacramental acts seems a mistake, the central Christian conviction remains secure. God is known best, not by separation from common things, but by such identification with them that we find the divine meaning latent in them. A vigorous religion will deal more with the home than with the church and more with the workbench than with the altar. The postman, binding separated people together, may be a kind of priest. Jesus taught His disciples how to pray, but He also taught them how to become better fishermen. Christ's use of parables is one application of the belief in a sacramental universe. The deepest truths about the human spirit could be expressed by reference to seeds and soils and birds and stones and lambs.

All who know something of the remarkable experiment being conducted by members of the Church of Scotland on the Island of Iona know that the restoration of the wholeness of life is basic to the undertaking. These modern men, who work with both hand and brain, and who unite prayer and labor in one frame of reference, are deeply inspired by the example of Columba who played so large a part in the conversion of Scotland to the Christian religion in the sixth century. They, too, are concerned with the "conversion of Scotland," and they are convinced that in the twentieth century as in the sixth, this will require more than preaching. What the Iona Community of our day says of Columba explains his own convictions and the convictions central to our present study.

> For him there was no department of man's activity that was not the province for the practical expression of the Christian ethic. He fulfilled in himself and in all he did that abiding sense of the oneness-of-all, the most significant emphasis in the Celtic Church. Religion was life; all life was holy, indivisible, the province for the fulfillment of the grace of God. Living was a sacrament, to pray was to work, to work was to pray. It was inevitable, therefore, that so practical a sense of religion, persistently pursued, tirelessly exercised, should have resulted in a greatly enhanced standard of life in all its branches, in agriculture, in learning, in art. . . . Their missions concerned the whole of life—the integration of the spiritual and the material; the cure of souls, the science of healing, the cultivation of land, the carving of wood, the building of houses and ships as well as of churches and monasteries, the wroughting of iron, the baking of bread, the work of smiths, of fishermen and hunters.[2]

There was one area, itself the most important of all, in which Columba and his associates failed to demonstrate

[2] *Behold Iona*, p. 7.

in their own experience the thrilling conviction about which their experience centered. They had no families! They would have been still greater men if they had identified themselves with common life to the extent of experiencing conjugal love, the procreation of children and the support of families. There are many good men and women who practice lifelong celibacy from religious motives or under a sense of vocation, but they are not illustrating the sacramental view of life at its highest point. It is a gross misuse of words to denote as "the religious" those who live in separation from common life, and it is especially pernicious to suppose that they represent some higher order of human excellence. On the contrary, if we take seriously the central convictions of the Christian religion, we must allow that married sanctity is superior. Many a harassed mother knows secrets of the devotional life that the men will never know. To worship God in a cloister is one thing, but to worship God amidst the insistent demands of husband and children is another. Each position has its hardships, but success in the latter constitutes the greater victory.

Most of us have been attracted, at one time or another, to the experimental fellowships which have been formed by separated communities in various centuries, including our own. Many, deeply impressed with the wickedness and complexity of the ordinary world, are tempted to go off with others of like mind and to form separated communities, such as those of the Hutterites, but this is a temptation to be resisted, because the separated community is not the highest ideal. Our fellowship must be *in* the world, not out of it. To go off with our own small group is really an escape and, though such escapes may keep something from being lost in very black times, they are not ordinarily what the world needs most. While the conception animating the original Franciscan orders was noble, that which animated the Third Order was nobler still, for it involved the effort to be true Franciscans while engaged in mundane pursuits as fathers and mothers and supporters of others.

Many of the experimental communities in America were of the separated type, an example being the Amana Colony in Iowa, but others were conducted in the midst of ordinary economic, political and domestic existence. One of the noblest of these was that of William Penn, who called his ambitious enterprise "an holy experiment in government." The experiment did not involve celibacy, as did the Shaker experiments, nor renunciation of private property, as did Amana, nor renunciation of political responsibility as have those of German pietists. Penn's was a holy experiment which was conducted while men carried on ordinary competition in what was frequently an unfriendly environment. In this regard Penn, though the nobler features of his plan were not maintained, has pointed out the way of advance. The fellowship we seek will usually constitute a minority, it will be a remnant, but it dare not be a separated remnant. Its witness must be made while living on streets and serving on city governments and supporting public schools. *The remnant cannot be a saving remnant unless it is attached to the main garment of our common life.*

It has always been recognized to some degree in Western civilization that the great moments of life, the birth of a baby, adolescence, marriage and death should be brought explicitly within the compass of the Christian fellowship. Man's greatest joys, as well as his sorrows and perplexities have been most appropriately recognized, we have agreed, in a religious setting. Baptism is the first entrance into the Christian community, confirmation is the self-conscious recognition of the experience of sharing in the fellowship, marriage is the public avowal, before the community, of the fidelity of one man and one woman, a recognition that the entire fellowship has a stake in the home about to be established. Death is the temporary loss of a member as he leaves the church militant. It is no wonder that acts at such times have been esteemed sacramental. These sacraments were not *invented*; they were *recognized* and *accepted.*

The degree to which the Church has included these high moments and helped men and women to experience them with reverence has been good. Sometimes this is all that has kept the Church alive in dull periods. We should, accordingly, learn from this and extend the principle much farther. The opening of a new home may be glorified by a special ceremony appropriate to the occasion. The dreams and efforts of a family, long anticipating its own home, deserve such recognition. A deed is often a sacred document representing countless hours of toil and saving. There is no worthy phase of human conduct that could not, with equal appropriateness, be brought under the canopy of the spiritual fellowship, for all real achievements of men deserve to be celebrated as occasions for thanksgiving. This has long been done in rural communities in harvest festivals, but the problem is to do something equally appropriate in urban centers. How difficult this may be is shown by the relative artificiality of our one nationally sponsored religious observance, Thanksgiving Day. Since most people now live in cities, Thanksgiving is chiefly a time when, before going to a football game, they merely have a bigger dinner than they usually enjoy.

The problem is to find the urban counterpart of the rural festivals. What is the equivalent, in a mechanical or industrial society, of a good harvest? Perhaps it is an invention, perhaps it is the completion of a new school building, perhaps it is the inauguration of a system of city parks or a program of slum clearance or municipal housing. In some areas it might be soil conservation. The fact that we do not think of these as religious occasions is our condemnation; it shows the degree to which we have allowed our lives to be departmentalized—and accordingly secularized. Religion, we suppose, has nothing to do with medical discoveries and with city planning. Religion, we suppose, is something that a few people have when they go to a half-darkened building on Sunday morning. And it is no wonder that the world thinks this, because the Church itself appears to think so, too. We have allowed our sacred fellowship to become an abstracted, departmental thing, because we have lacked the imagination to make it truly universal in scope. The periods of our Western history in which the Church has been the chief regenerating force in civilization have been those in which the total character of the Christian Society has been recognized. The Church, when so understood, becomes quite naturally the Mother of the Arts, the inspirer of natural science and the spiritual support of the law. Now we have sunk so far that many people suppose there is a necessary antagonism between the Church and these cultural children which she spawned long ago.[3]

When we begin to think of what can be done to demonstrate the total character of the Christian fellowship, there seems to be no limit to what might be done. The task is to take the spiritual life people already have and dignify that by including it in a wider setting rather than to scold men because of what they do not have. The kind of idealism that goes into the Farm Bureau Movement or the Labor Union would be brought under the canopy and thereby enhanced if we were really successful. The fact that so few members of labor unions suppose there is any vital link between themselves and any church is a standing criticism of all who have the enlargement of the Christian fellowship at heart. Churches, these people suppose, are for owners and white-collar workers. We do not see how to solve this problem, but we can be very sure that it will have to be solved before religion again becomes a truly integrating and renewing experience in the modern world.

If we take seriously our central conviction that religion is not something separate from ordinary life, but a divine frame into which all ordinary events can be placed, we begin to see practical applications of importance for our culture. What, for instance, is a Christian college or a Christian university? It is not merely an institution founded under Christian auspices and by Christian inspiration, for nothing is easier than to depart from such a foundation

[3] The supposed cleavage between religion and science has been greatly exaggerated and is largely a modern innovation. For the most part it is not more than a hundred years old and is, we trust, already disappearing as an unhappy interlude.

while keeping the same name and the same official statement of purpose. It is not an institution which has, at some one point in its curriculum, a course in the Bible or in the history of Christian thought, valuable as these courses may be. Such courses can be given without marked effect on the total academic undertaking.

If our view of religion is correct a Christian college is one in which every department is marked by conscious and unapologetic commitment to the Christian life. Each professor in such a college must meet two requirements, both of which are equally necessary: he must be academically *competent* and he must be religiously *committed*. The Christian religion, not being merely spiritual, is as much interested in the way chemistry and astronomy are taught as in the way philosophy and religion are taught. The trustees, being themselves committed men, will seek to find competent physicists and historians and psychologists who will approach their subjects and their students in a mood of deep reverence. It will not be necessary for them to open their lectures with prayer, because their reverent attitude will shine through all that they do and say. It will appear both in their humility in the face of the fundamental mysteries and in their loyal acceptance of evidence which happens to controvert their pet theories.

It is frequently in science that we find some of the most powerful potential religion of our time. Not only may the very fact of science be employed as the first great reason for believing in God, as the late Archbishop Temple has done so persuasively,[4] but the vocation of the scientist may be one of the most devout of human enterprise. There

[4] Cf. William Temple, *Nature, Man and God,* chap. V.

have been a number of nontheistic scientists in our own unhappy day, but they do not represent the major tradition. The major tradition was represented by Agazziz when he would begin a demonstration experiment by saying, "Gentlemen, we shall now seek to know God's thoughts after Him." What makes the action so devout, potentially, is the rigorous honesty, and the exacting care. Many of those who have posed as experts in religion have not had this same exactitude or self-discipline, while a laboratory may be a school of piety.

The day of the cocksure scientist who knew there was nothing to the idea of revelation because it had never been demonstrated in the laboratory is now over. Many modern scentists are among the humblest of men, partly because they are among the most frightened of men, but also because real depth of scientific experience tends to make the ultimate mystery more baffling. The testimony of the most distinguished of the modern historians of science deserves a wider reading than it has received. Dr. Sarton writes:

> In spite of scientific progress or rather because of it, nothing is more needed today than humility and reverence,—humility induced by the ever-increasing mysteries of life, by our ignorance of fundamentals, by our lack of appreciation of the infinite beauty surrounding us; reverence for the accomplishments of good men and good women throughout the centuries all over the world.[5]

The practical achievements of science lend themselves to a sense of reverent thanks more than almost any other factor in our experience. The work of Allen and Doisy in isolating and identifying estrogen, and thereby making

[5] George Sarton, *The Albert Schweitzer Jubilee Book*, p. 46.

way for the relief of pain or disappointment in the lives of countless women, is a case in point. Such men go through years of patient and seemingly unrewarding labor, but the results may be tremendous in the alleviation of human ills for millions yet unborn. How reasonable it would be, if we saw our Christian faith in its fullness, to enter such exacting labor with a prayer on our lips and to end it with thanksgiving! Our science would then not only be good religion; it would also be better science.

The most remarkable feature of the devotional life of the great Dr. Samuel Johnson is at precisely this point. The prayers for which he is best remembered are not those composed in church, but those composed as he faced new and exacting tasks. He began his famous *Dictionary* in a mood of reverent prayer and he began his periodical essays in the same way. To the world these may have seemed like secular pursuits, but to a man of Johnson's convictions the word "secular" hardly had any meaning. The entrance upon the study of law was the occasion of prayer as naturally as was the entrance upon the study of religion.

There, then, is our clue. The Christian faith must rediscover its own essential genius, which is the union of the secular and the sacred, of matter and of spirit, the common and the divine. If the Christian Church is to regain its hold on the life of modern man it must find ways of meeting people where their interests lie, and this requires disciplined imagination. We have to *think*, if we are to know how to do it. The task of those who feel a sense of responsibility for the work of the Church is not to condemn the present lack of spirituality nor to wring their hands over the wickedness of the contemporary world, but to be on the lookout for the meaning already inherent in the life men now know, and to find ways of enhancing this meaning by lifting it up into a context of divine love.

The differences in human life depend, for the most part, not on what men *do*, but upon the meaning and purpose of their acts. All are *born*, all *die*, all *lose their loved ones*, nearly all *marry* and nearly all *work*, but the *significance* of these acts may vary enormously. The same physical act may be in one situation vulgar and in another holy. The same work may be elevating or degrading. The major question is not, "What act do I perform?" but "In what frame do I put it?" Wisdom about life consists in taking the inevitable ventures which are the very stuff of common existence, and glorifying them.

CHAPTER II

Marriage

Animals have not to manage a household.

ARISTOTLE

OF ALL human events, none more easily becomes an occasion for rejoicing than does marriage. Death is solemnizing, but marriage is both solemnizing and joyous at the same moment. Even the dullest person alive can hardly fail to have a sense of wonder as he sees a man and woman take their places before an altar and pledge their lifelong devotion to each other. Much of the art and much of the science of our world are efforts to find unity in diversity, the artist suffusing an entire scene with a single mood and the scientist finding a single law demonstrated in apparently diverse phenomena, but every marriage goes further. Marriage not only *discovers* unity; it undertakes to *create* unity, and to create in the most important areas of experience.

Two lives, belonging to different sexes, and often with widely different biological background, come together in the sight of God and before their friends to inaugurate something never seen in the world before—their particular combination of inheritance and their particular union of personalities. They join their destinies in such a manner that sorrow for one will be sorrow for the other and good fortune for one will be good fortune for the other. Moreover, both they and their friends are keenly aware that the normally expected result of their union will be the coming into the world of new persons, who, apart from this union, would never have been granted the boon of existence.

It is this overpowering sense of *possibility* that makes even the most unostentatious wedding so moving an occasion. Those who join their destinies in marriage are, by their very togetherness, sharing in the entire creative process in a unique way. Marriage is a window through which the meaning of human existence shines with unusual brilliance, and the window can never be so smudged that it wholly excludes that light.

We understand better the way in which marriage is fraught with tremendous possibility when we think of its range of failure and success as well as its potential pains and joys. It is perfectly clear, on the one hand, that the possibility of sorrow is greater in married life than in single life. The outcome may range from that of the death of one partner or the failure of affection which is worse than death, to the glory of continual growth in creative union. Each person who marries opens himself voluntarily to pain, because he puts himself in a position in which he can more easily be hurt. The person who has not made the wager of devotion cannot be hurt by the unfaithfulness of another as can the person who makes the leap of faith. Every avowed lover is terribly vulnerable, and marriage only accentuates the vulnerability as it accentuates the possible glory. The married woman, especially if she is carrying a child, has put herself in a position of grave economic inequality in case her husband should abandon her without support. Her life would have been far easier, in every way, had she never married. Those who never gamble cannot lose.

Sometimes married life, instead of bringing these sharp pains, brings something which may, in the end, be worse: the constant mutual nagging of persons whose lives are unsuited to one another or who are unwilling to undergo the disciplines of character which successful marriage requires. What Thoreau said about his neighbors with their lives of "quiet desperation" applies to many marriages which do not end in the public failure which we call divorce, but continue unhappily and ingloriously until one partner dies. The truth is that many are worse off in the married state than they would have been if they had remained single, for while the married life can be far happier than the single life, it can also be far more wretched. Those who wish to avoid all risk are advised to remain single.

Among the many pitfalls and dangers of marriage the economic difficulty is often the most conspicuous, because the money question is hard for both the man and the woman. A man who has had only himself to support, suddenly has another and soon there may be more. It is easy for him to suppose that his wife is always thinking up some new expenditure just when he is trying hardest to save or to make ends meet. The economic problem may be even harder for the wife, who, prior to marriage, may have had money of her own and now suddenly finds herself dependent upon another, whom she must ask for whatever she needs. Frequently she is irked by the implied requirement of a strict accounting of funds. Though we might expect this problem to be greatest among the poor, wealth seems to be no real security against economic misunderstanding.

Both of the partners give up a great deal when they unite their lives. The woman usually gives up further chance for academic training and worldly independence. Especially after children come along, it is idle to speak of her as free to do whatever she likes. Frequently she is so encumbered with trivial and even menial duties that she feels she has no opportunity to keep up her intellectual interests. At the same time the man gives up much. He, too, if he takes marriage seriously or honorably, must limit his former freedom of movement. He can no longer give his entire attention to his business or profession, for marriage, if it is to succeed, also requires steady attention. The married man, in most instances, cannot expect the physical ease or quiet which the bachelor knows, and he cannot honorably engage in some highly dangerous pursuits. For example, a man who is devoted to mountain climbing is well advised to climb the most dangerous peaks *before* marriage.

When we think of the price which marriage demands and the countless pitfalls it involves, it is no wonder that there are some failures. The wonder is that there are not more! But this is only part, and the lesser part of the story. If married life can sink low in disloyalty and constant quarreling, it can also rise to majestic heights and *frequently does*. Many couples, whose names never appear in the headlines, live together radiantly for years so that final separation is the most cruel of blows. The glory of marriage is often seen in fidelity to a deceased partner like that of Doctor Samuel Johnson who was still remembering his wife in prayer after she had been dead for thirty years. It is also seen in fidelity in the face of physical separation, well illustrated by couples involuntarily separated during the war. One young man, kept from his wife for more than eight years by the war and its aftermath, when asked if the experience were not terribly hard, replied that he was helped by the story in Genesis of how Jacob waited seven years for Rachel, "and they seemed to him but a few days, because he loved her."

Because marriage reaches so deeply into the fundamentals of human experience and is so important a revelation of the grace of God, it is relatively independent of changing manners and customs. Accordingly the best statements of its meaning may be very old. One of the best is that of Jeremy Taylor nearly three hundred years ago:

> Marriage is a school and exercise of virtue; and though marriage hath cares, yet the single life hath desires, which are more troublesome and more dangerous, and often end in sin; while the cares are but instances of duty and exercises of piety; and therefore, if single life hath more privacy of devotion, yet marriage hath more necessities and more variety of it, and is an exercise of more graces. . . . Here is the proper scene of piety and patience, of the duty of parents, and the charity of relatives; here kindness is spread abroad, and love is united, and made firm as a centre: marriage is the nursery of heaven. . . . It lies under more burdens [than does the single life], but is supported by all the strengths of love and charity, and those burdens are delightful. Marriage is the mother of the world, and preserves kingdoms of the world, and fills cities, and churches, and heaven itself. . . .

Single life makes men in one instance to be like angels, but marriage in very many things makes the chaste pair to be like to Christ.[1]

What will help our uprooted generation most, in facing marriage, is to understand something of its essential meaning. Thousands of marriages fail because the participants have had no clear idea in advance of what their undertaking involves. The first essential of marriage is the acceptance, in advance, of the relationship as *unconditional*. The participants in the marriage service pledge themselves "for better and for worse." Frankly recognizing the dangers, the standardized service explicitly rejects the notion that these are sufficient to dissolve the union. There may be economic difficulties facing the young couple in the ensuing years and there may be real poverty, but the partners envisage this in advance when they take each other "for richer, for poorer." One partner may become ill, one may be unable to become a parent, but this eventuality is envisaged too; they take each other "in sickness and in health." Far from being a temporary affair, the troth is pledged "so long as we both shall live" or "till death shall separate us." And there are some bold couples, sensing the centrality of the unconditional, who here substitute the word "forever."

The point of all this is that marriage is not a contract. If it were a contract, it would cease to be in effect for one party once the other party failed to keep his side of the bargain. Instead of a contract it is a *commitment* and thus intrinsically religious, since commitment is the crucial step of religious experience. Faith is not mere intellectual assent, but the supreme gamble in which we stake our lives

[1] Jeremy Taylor, *Sermon on the Marriage Ring.*

upon a conviction. To believe that water will support our weight is one thing, but to trust our lives to it is another. The former is mere belief, but the latter is the commitment which is the heart of faith, and it is faith of this kind which marriage exemplifies.

It is only when marriage goes beyond the status of contract or a relation of temporary convenience that the true glory of the relationship is revealed. True religion, said Donald Hankey, is "betting your life that there is a God." Likewise we may say, "True marriage is betting your life that glorious union with your mate is possible." It is some sense of this meaning which causes so many people, including millions who are normally out of touch with organized religion, to try to make the marriage of their loved ones a religious occasion. They know that the highest things belong together; they are sufficiently sensitive to realize that there is at least one human undertaking which is debased if it is wholly secularized. Men who never pray, who spend their Sundays on the golf course, who never read their Bibles, and who do not even support a church financially, will go to almost any length to provide their daughters with church weddings.

The spectacle of the pagan families insisting on church weddings is very instructive. It shows that we are not willing to take our paganism straight! If all men were as the modern pagan is, there would be no churches in which to have such weddings, there would be no marriage service with its noble mood of commitment, and there would be nobody to perform it. But inconsistency does not seem to bother some men. They even suppose that they are doing the church a kind of honor by using its facilities, and they think that those facilities ought to be there waiting whenever they wish to employ them. This means, of course, that they misunderstand the nature of the church, that they do not appreciate that the central reality is the fellowship, rather than the building or the ceremonies or the services rendered. Apparently thousands suppose that a church is like a business house or a public hotel where one pays for goods or services as demanded. Nothing, however, could be farther from the truth.

For those who are willing for the whole of life, including marriage, to be secularized, there is a way provided. They can go to a justice of the peace to have a civil marriage which, in our culture, is wholly legal. Of course it is unaesthetic, of course it is a frankly commercial undertaking, but that is what they ought to expect. The men who make their living by performing such civil marriages are easy to find, since they often live close to the courthouse and frequently display electric signs announcing the presence of "marriage parlors."

In order to avoid possible misunderstanding it is important to add a relevant remark at this point, to the effect that the marriage before a civil official *may* be a devout occasion and the resultant union may be a thing of beauty in spite of its drab beginnings, for marriage is potentially so wonderful that it can overcome many severe handicaps. There are thousands of couples, married before a justice, who, in spite of the secular surroundings and words, make their act deeply devout and sacramental. In fact, some civil marriages are far more religious than are some marriages in churches, particularly those in which the dominant motive is the desire to be fashionable or even ostentatious.

Consider a marriage in a home or in a garden. This may be an occasion of great beauty and, sometimes, of genuine reverence, but the problem before those eager to retain and emphasize the sacred aspect is very great. Often, in a home, the guests press closely on one another in necessarily crowded quarters and deep silence is almost impossible. The people have been laughing and joking, as they have a right to do in a home, until the very moment the service begins. Sometimes the good things to eat are conspicuously present and people know that one kind of service will follow the other. The household servants may even be at the doors with trays of champagne, waiting for the last public words to be said. Ministers may be so wedged between the people on the stairway and the people in the hall that they hardly have room to move. It is not impossible to conduct a service of worship in such circumstances, but it is very hard, and the minister usually knows when he has failed. It is very hard to keep the sacred words from sounding perfunctory.

Even in a church a wedding may easily fail to rise to the high level of sacramental experience. Marriage, especially the church marriage, has so interwoven the fashionable with the spiritual that the former is always close to the surface. The temptation is to be so concerned with the details of fashionable correctness that the inner meaning is lost. People whose major attention is given to the neckties for the ushers and flowers for the bridesmaids have little mind left for a proper consideration of the significance of the primary act.

It is interesting to note the way in which the cinema usually depicts a church wedding as an essentially fashionable occasion rather than a religious one. The clergyman must, of course, be present, but his part is plainly secondary and he is represented as saying the words as a functionary rather than one who is leading in a genuine act of worship.

What makes marriage sacred rather than secular is not some particular form of priestly words and certainly not some hocus pocus, but what is in the hearts of those participating in the momentous event. The truth is that any marriage *can* be religious, regardless of secular surroundings, just as any marriage *can* be crassly secular, regardless of ecclesiastical surroundings. The reality of marriage depends on the inner experience of the man and woman who marry and not on any external act or words, no matter how symbolic. The justice or the priest cannot join them, for God alone can do that, and all the officiating person can do is to give voice to what is already an interior fact.

This emphasis on the interior reality leads to consideration of the second essential of the marriage relationship. If it is the inner reality that counts, why do we need any ceremony at all? Why should not the man and woman who are committed to lifelong fidelity begin living together without further ado and avoid all the bother? The answer is that, because the community has a stake in the creative union and deserves the joy of participation, the full meaning of the step cannot be realized unless its public character is understood. Private or secret marriage is a contradiction in terms, and the quick marriage is always a failure to appreciate the total situation.[2]

[2] Cf. *The Book of Church Order*, of the Presbyterian Church in the United States, chap. XIII. "Marriage is of a public nature. The welfare of civil society, the happiness of families, and the credit of religion, are deeply interested in it. Therefore, the purpose of marriage should be sufficiently published a proper time previous to the solemnization of it."

Marriage, according to the dominant Christian pattern, is a recognition of the deep fact of *community*. It says, in vivid language, that Christians are members one of another. People who fall in love could go off and begin living together if they chose, but they would, by so doing, be disloyal to the conception of the Beloved Community. What we hold is that love is so sacred that it ought not to be consummated lightly, but should receive the blessing of the group of those who care. The miracle happens, not at the altar, but when two people realize that fullness of life for them involves a complete unity of destiny. What happens at the altar is that the stamp of approval of the Christian community is made. A wedding is a religious occasion during which a man and woman make vows of lifelong fidelity, in the presence of those whose approbation they prize and whose blessing they seek.

Such an understanding of the nature of marriage helps us to see what is wrong with the marriage at the office of the justice of the peace or in the study of the free-lance minister. That kind of marriage is spiritually impoverished because it is detached and broken. It is torn away from the fabric of our culture. This isolation from the participating community, seen at its worst in the quick marriage, whether before a justice or a clergyman, symbolizes one of the most unhappy features of our modern urban civilization. It is characteristic of a culture in which people do not know their neighbors in the next apartment. In a simpler and more rural life the courtship of a couple is observed by friends and neighbors, usually with joyous anticipation. Finally comes the time for marriage, which is quite naturally celebrated in the village church or meeting house in the presence of the community. All belong to the community and the community puts its stamp of approval upon what the members do. But those who go to some Gretna Green to begin the union of their destinies are denying themselves all this sense of communal participation. Their action is only a natural symptom of the degree to which the wholeness of life has already been destroyed in our modern experience, but it is nevertheless unfortunate.

The difficulty with so many modern marriages is that they lack *reality*; they are largely fictions. The man who pronounces the couple man and wife has never seen them before and may never see them again; the witnesses care nothing about them and have made no inquiry into the suitability of the union they are witnessing. Usually vows are not even repeated, but the couple's participation is reduced to the hurried and banal "I do." The difference between this and common law marriage is not very great, the chief difference being some kind of record. It is not surprising that couples, looking back on such a transaction in later years, frequently feel cheated. They realize that they have made so little of what might have been so much. One such couple came later to a beautiful church and asked permission to stand before the altar to say their vows to each other in a setting which seemed to them requisite to their glorious commitment. "We know we are legally married already," they said, "but this will be *real*."

It is one of the prices of our freedom that the right to perform religious marriages is held by some whose credentials would not be respected by the churches of the major tradition. As long as any little sect has "ordained" a man and his ordination has not been revoked, there is no solution of this problem. Men of this type sometimes gravitate to border towns where the quick marriages are performed and some of them have no congregations. In this situation the fact that they call themselves ministers does not necessarily make the marriages they perform more truly religious occasions than are the civil procedures. The service may be as brief, there may be the same circumvention of the requirement of the presence of witnesses, there may be the same commercial motive, there may be the same separation from the participating community. In some ways this is worse than the frankly civil marriage, because it is less honest. It claims to be something which it is not.

One small straw in the contemporary wind is the appearance of the House of Marriage. This is the counterpart of the Funeral Parlor and clearly inspired by the latter's success. Whether the House of Marriage idea will grow we do not know, but we are wise to remember that the Funeral Parlor, though now a firmly entrenched institution, fully accepted by the majority, is a modern innovation. The still newer institution could provide everything from ring to flowers to music to clergyman. Since three of these are already provided by funeral establishments, it would be easy for the same establishment to provide both kinds of service. Thus marriage, like death, would be placed on a secure financial basis! The father of the bride could go in advance and arrange for the covering charge and the House Minister would be paid a salary. This would be an efficient and sensible system and might come to be taken for granted in a civilization in which the Church is seen more and more as an anachronism.

The system would be efficient, but it would be terribly vulgar and much of the glory of marriage would inevitably be lost thereby. The hired clergyman of the House of Death and Marriage would not be a real minister because he would serve no congregation. There would be no *koinonia* to which he would be responsive. The service would not be religious, but merely sentimental.

A less vulgar step in this direction is made possible by the chapels found in some cemeteries, of which the most highly publicized is situated in Los Angeles. Many are married in such buildings in the supposition that they are thereby having "church weddings." The buildings *look* like churches, but they are *not* churches, for they are not the scenes of worshiping congregations. The real church is the living fellowship, but these buildings were not constructed by the sacrifice of the members of the fellowship. They were constructed by hard-headed financiers with an eye for good business.

There is even danger, today, that actual churches may lend their support to the commercialization of marriage and thus to the destruction of something infinitely precious in our common life. There are some great city churches which today arrange for weddings on the basis of the overall charge. Thus it is possible to have a hundred dollar wedding, a fifty dollar wedding or a twenty-five dollar wedding. It all depends on the amount and kind of music and the relative grandeur of the setting. It is doubtful whether those who have encouraged this development have any idea how dangerous it is. Whatever the words they say and however grand the vestments, they are aiding rather than opposing the secularizing tendency of our time.

The secularization of marriage, whether in the court house, the marriage parlor or the church, is a barometer of civilization. The enormous increase in divorce indicates the degree to which marriage has been looked upon as a contractual rather than a sacramental relation. This helps us to know where to put our emphasis if we care about the revival or continuance of something superlatively good. If marriage, in the sense of commitment, should be lost by any generation, it would be exceedingly difficult to reproduce it. Without marriage in the sense of lifelong fidelity and mutual parental responsibility, the race would undoubtedly go on, but there is little likelihood that it would go on well. There would still be mating and there would still be children, but the most precious of intangibles would be lost. To recognize this is to understand something of our task.

Our present task is to help as many young persons as possible to a true understanding of marriage and to its continuing possibilities. They will be helped if they realize that marriage, not only on the wedding day, but in its entire course, is a public affair. If we take seriously the essentially public nature of marriage, the clear implication is that we must give the encompassing community a larger share in the undertaking. The chief way in which this may be done is by seeking the approval of the worshiping community well in advance. A step in this direction is the announcement of intentions or publishing of bans. Where this is required the sudden midnight ceremony in the house of a stranger is, of course, impossible. The experience of the Society of Friends, during the last three hundred years, may be profitable to other groups at this point. In a Quaker wedding the stake of the entire group is recognized from the beginning in that the couple intending marriage bring forth their proposal to a monthly meeting of their fellow members. If the union seems, under a sense of divine guidance, to be in good order, the marriage is allowed and a date set for it. Usually time is given for a committee to present a report a month later, so that a sudden wedding is impossible. When the day of the wedding arrives, the couple say their vows of fidelity before their friends and fellow members, a number of whom sign the certificate as having witnessed the vows. Thus there is no need of a clergyman or officiating minister. The conviction is that there is nothing which such a person could add, for the central fact has already occurred. The public nature of marriage is taken so seriously that the stamp of approval is that, not of one man, but of the group itself. That such an experience often reaches great heights of reverence and high seriousness goes without saying. But something of this character can also be caught by others who follow different procedures.

The simplicity and directness of the Quaker marriage vows, as they arise spontaneously out of a setting of profound silence may also be a model for others. "In the presence of the Lord and before these friends, I, John, take thee Mary, to be my wife, promising, with divine assistance, to be unto thee a loving and faithful husband so long as we both shall live." Whether this or the vow found in the *Book of Common Prayer* is used, there is little doubt that any marriage service is deepened if the bride and groom learn their own vows and say them without prompting. This takes us one step farther away from the banal "I do" and provides something beautiful to remember and repeat in subsequent days. Moreover the mutual task of learning the vows in advance is a beneficent experience. *It is beneficent because it extends the period during which the couple are made conscious of the religious aspect of their union.*

Though the ideal plan of advance announcement to the worshiping group will not be followed by most people in our day, partly because there are so many who are not members of any worshiping group, and partly because so many are geographically uprooted, a step in this same helpful direction is made possible by the growing practice among sensitve clergymen of demanding one or more long interviews before the wedding day. Many married people now say that, though they cannot remember what they said, or what anyone else said, as they stood before the altar, they *can* remember vividly and gratefully what the minister said as he talked with them in a quiet and leisurely manner in his study. This is the minister's great chance. The young hearts are open; they are unusually receptive to high ideals; they recognize the religious nature of their total act. Here is the chance to help to set standards for years, to inspire high hopes, to give advice that will carry them over many hard places. It is vastly important in this connection that the minister's own married life should be a thing of joy and glory, wholly above reproach. If he has failed in his own enterprise his words to the young will have a hollow ring, but, if he can say, "We did it this way and it worked," he may perform a truly noble service. One test of his spiritual integrity will be his own sense of excitement. If he is the man he ought to be, he cannot face the young couple before him in his study without something very much like tears in his eyes, even though he has faced a hundred other such couples before. Only those who are very dull can contemplate any marriage without deep emotion and a minister who is dull is in the wrong work. The sensitive adviser will see the pain of possible separation, the wonder of babies which belong to both, and the possible years of joyful work together. He will also see the possible tragedy of failure with the production of bitterness greater than is known in other human relationships. It is no wonder that the minister prays with the young couple; no other expression is adequate.

The chief way in which the glory of the marriage bond can be maintained in our highly secularized culture is by making the whole undertaking unapologetically and frankly religious. We must lift the whole experience into the mood of reverence and dedication, without which the best rewards will never be appropriated or their existence even suspected. As in both art and science, there are definite preconditions of awareness, and the chief condition seems to be the mood of reverent commitment. This often turns what might have been crass and prosaic into a relationship of steady wonder.

In conventional novels, a couple falls deeply in love and then marriage follows as a mere consequence, bringing the story to an end. In actual life it is the other way; often the deepest love comes after marriage rather than before and is clearly its consequence. Before marriage there may be romantic attachment, but marriage itself can produce a relationship of infinitely greater depth and creative power. Marriage is magic in many lives, partly because it combines the flesh and the spirit in such a remarkable unity. Sexual experience is glorified by its spiritual setting and identification of destiny is made concrete by the practice of the closest physical intimacy that is possible for men and women. The mere sex act outside of the encompassing sense of spiritual community becomes relatively meaningless, while Platonic affection without the material sign of that community becomes an abstraction.

A great deal of nonsense has been written in our day about sexual "adjustment." Of course there are persons who, through no fault of their own, are not adequately equipped for the physical side of marriage, but these are rare, indeed. There are thousands of women with whom any normal man might find satisfactory sexual relations, so far as the physical aspect is considered, and there are thousands of men with whom any normal woman might find such satisfaction. We are finding an excuse that is too easy when we blame failure on "sexual maladjustment," as is so often done in divorce cases. Our real difficulty usually lies in the realm of significance, in the capacity for glorification of common acts, in the provision of an adequate spiritual framework. In short, a vast amount of sexual failure is failure to attain to the level of the sacramental. Even on the level of sexual enjoyment the mere materialist, like the mere spiritualist, is an unfortunate person, to be pitied. He misses the best.

If marriage is to be maintained at this high level of mutual responsibility and mutual profit, the sacred aspect must be continued throughout its entire course. It is a mistake to think of sacramental marriage as something which occurs one June day and is then over. Two people are not "married" in the ceremony of an hour; they only *begin* to be married, and what is then begun can continue, with growing meaning, as long as life lasts. We ought to provide ways of calling this important, but easily neglected, fact to our attention, since men and women are creatures who need constant reminders, even of those truths which they deeply believe. One way of providing a reminder is to frame the marriage certificate and hang it in a prominent place in the new home that is formed. This certificate is especially valuable if it includes the signatures of a number of witnesses who are much loved and whose good will and approbation the couple prizes. Then their success or failure seem to be surrounded by a cloud of witnesses. The couple can also be helped in their sacred enterprise by employing times of family worship or grace at table as occasions of thanksgiving to God for their union and prayer for its continuous success. Married couples should pray every morning of their married lives for the revelation of new glory in the events of the day and for the deepening of their love, one to another. Soon this mood can become a genuine habit, so that it is never far below the surface of consciousness.

The most difficult hurdle for countless young couples is the economic one mentioned earlier in this chapter. The homes in which the problem of making ends meet each month is the paramount issue, probably constitute the majority. When money is scarce and needs apparently so great, it is alarmingly easy for the couple to fall into the habit of mutual recrimination. The young husband feels that he is being criticized because his earning power is so low, while the young wife feels that she is being accused of wastefulness of resources. They see others who seem to have everything easy and envy fills their hearts. Soon they say hard words to each other which may do lasting harm and the precious but relatively fragile relationship called marriage is broken. Years of glorified happiness are thus sacrificed.

We may as well admit that there is no easy or simple solution to this problem of money. It is probable that, to the end of time, most people will desire or actually need more than they have. Most couples will have hard financial sledding for the first fifteen years of married existence and millions will have such difficulty until they cease to breathe. But, though the problem cannot have a full solution, it can be mitigated, and that in two distinct ways. First, a great deal of the pressure can be removed by the conscious adoption of a plan of simplicity in living. If simplicity is adopted as an ideal and not merely a grim necessity, it is not so galling. Thoreau, we must remember, had no financial worries while he lived at Walden Pond. He found that many things which people suppose they need are not necessary at all. They go through life, pushing in front of them a house and barn and a hundred acres of land, often making themselves servants to the farm. It will, of course, be noted with justice that Thoreau's problem was far easier than that of the married couple, since he had neither wife nor child. But, after we have made this concession, the message of Walden is still highly relevant. In our modern existence we are tempted to increase our mechanical standard of living each year and always to keep it ahead of our resources. We are then panting to catch up and the very satisfaction which our possessions ought to provide us is lost in the struggle to pay for them. One of the grandest things that could be done for the success of marriage in the modern world would be the recovery of simplicity as a Christian ideal.

The second important thing to say about the economic problem is that it can be approached in the mood and context of religious faith. A wise young couple will know that they are going to be poor a long time, they will sense the dangers which this situation involves, and they will seek a solution in the spirit of prayer. They will see this as one of the chief tests of their mutual loyalty and they will endeavor to meet the test *together*. It will not be the man's problem and not the woman's problem, but it will be their *joint* problem. They may even come to see it as a *challenge* and be strengthened by it. They may come to be glad that they live in the real world of financial hardship rather than the cloud-cuckoo land of the playboy millionaire. Above all they may come to appreciate, in their struggle, the sacramental aspect of money. Money, from one point of view, is terribly crass, the essence of a materialistic civilization, but from another point of view it is the possibility of human welfare. The same ten dollar bill can be wasted by gambling with it on the horse race, or it may be used to send supplies to some needy family in Europe. But the same ten dollars cannot do both! It is either or, and this very disjunction gives a solemn and sacred aspect to its use. If the young couple, in spite of their relative poverty, can be so careful in expenditures that they are able to help others, even in tiny amounts, then their enterprise has already been lifted out of the prosy business of pinching pennies into the glorified one of a truly sacramental experience. Though the love of money is the root of all evil, the right employment of money is a high and holy task. The young wife, who handles her husband's meager wages, is sharing in a glorious undertaking and her entire marriage will be lifted up by the knowledge that this is so.

The dangers of failure in marriage have always been great, but the dangers are vastly accentuated in our modern industrialized existence. For millions, there is no real stake in the community, no sense of belonging and no group whose approbation is highly valued. This last point is so important that it can hardly be exaggerated. When people can move away so easily the desire for approbation, which has heretofore been one of the chief civilizing forces, loses most of its power.

The dangers which married life faces are so great that only a strong moral sense can succeed. In most lives this does not appear except under a sense of religious motivation. Mere physical attractiveness will not suffice. One evidence that this is true is the fact that the part of our country which is admitted to have the highest concentration of physical beauty, both male and female, is the part of the country most notorious for marriage failures. Economic bonds will not suffice, for people can find ways out of them. But the love of God *will* suffice. The one setting in which the union of two lives is most likely to succeed is that of prayer. This is so much a matter of common sense that eventually we may come to realize its truth.

CHAPTER III

Birth

Children are your riches; and upon their turning out well or ill depends the whole order of their father's house.

PLATO

MEN and women who are joined in wedlock according to the *Book of Common Prayer* are reminded, during the public service itself, that the normal expectation of their union is children, and that the coming of such children will involve their parents in a solemn responsibility for their care. Only the prudish think this indelicate. Not all people who marry are *able* to have children, but marriage without the *hope* of children is no marriage. Couples who value inordinately their own ease, who wish to sleep all night without the disturbance of infants, and who desire to keep their homes in perfect order, naturally fear the introduction of children into their lives, and some resist their coming for these reasons. But these are never really good homes, even though they may be orderly and neat in outward appearance. Frequently such homes go on the rocks of internal discord and this is what we ought to expect, since love of ease is a weak human bond. As men and women grow older, losing some of their physical attractiveness, their lives need powerful connecting links, and the most powerful of all human links is children who belong to both and who have been brought into existence through the mutual love of both parents. One of the really encouraging signs of our time is the fact that so many young couples, when approaching marriage, now talk frankly, though not lightly, of their hope of children.

Throughout all of our known history, birth has been looked upon as a religious event. Life is full of crises, but man seems to have realized early that a crisis may be a means of divine revelation. Birth and death are such crises, and they are equally mystifying. The notion of an end is solemn, but the notion of a beginning is equally solemn. Once there was not this new person at all, and now he is alive, with years of varied experience before him. He is a unique combination of factors, never seen in the world before and this tiny body is destined to be intertwined with a responsible soul, capable of knowing God and sensitive to the call of duty. If a sacrament is a way of intertwining the material and the spiritual so that new grace emerges, the birth of any baby is surely sacramental for all who can appreciate it.

All sensitive parents realize that their baby is a sheer gift. They have had, nine months earlier, some small part in the production of the tiny body, but this seems almost trivial in relationship to the entire event. Fathers and mothers cannot *make* a life; at best they can be instruments of its emergence. We can help, in minor ways, to provide a good physical environment, including nourishment, but we cannot make anything *grow*. We cannot even heal; the best that we can do in this regard is to try to eliminate some of the factors which hinder or retard the healing process, which is something *given*. Accordingly the wise parents look at the little bundle of flesh and say to themselves that this is really a little stranger. He isn't even *theirs*, though he is their responsibility for a few years. They are given the high privilege of guiding his life, protecting him from various dangers and watching him develop into a true man. Adequate recognition of this makes the crisis called birth not merely a natural event, but a religious event also. To be allowed to guide the life of a child is to be given an *incredible compliment*. It means that we are trusted with the responsibility of forming characters which may have eternal significance. No sensitive person can face this relationship without a deep sense of unworthiness as well as of honest reverence.

Much of the religious consciousness surrounding birth arises from the keen sense of potentiality. We look at the babies in the maternity hospital, each lying in a basket, and each with an identification label. Here is "McFadden Girl" and there is "Cohen Boy." What is in store for these new people? Some will meet disappointment and opposition and pain, for we cannot shield them always or even long. As we look at their little red faces we begin to think of all the joy and wonder that may be in store for them. Some of them may affect deeply, for good or ill, the fortunes and destinies of countless other persons, and some may bring to the world new thoughts of which we have not yet dreamed. We have made a pretty bad mess of the old world, but as long as there are new babies there is hope.

How little could the observers in the Kentucky cabin and in the English country house, on February 12, 1809, have realized the possibilities in the tiny bundles before them!

It is in some such mood as this that people turn to organized religion to try to say or do something worthy of an event so momentous. Thus arises the practice of infant baptism or of christening. It is noteworthy that many of those who, in the past, have borne a strong testimony against infant baptism, tend now to have something analogous to it. In the past they have opposed infant baptism on the conviction that baptism, symbolizing the entrance into the new life of union with Christ, cannot have meaning and reality unless it results from a conscious choice of a responsible person, something of which no infant is capable. Others have recognized the dangers which come from the practice of infant baptism, especially the supposition that the mere external act has some kind of magical efficacy. We see how easily this leads to superstition, and we know that superstition is the enemy of true religion. But many Christian groups, while keeping these convictions, and sensing the dangers, have introduced the practice of bringing parents with new babies before the congregation, asking them to dedicate their children to Christian living and to endeavor to bring them up in the nurture of the worshiping community. This is not outward baptism, but it serves the purpose which others find in actual christening. It provides a public recognition that birth is sacred, that children are divine gifts, and that the responsibility of parents is a highly religious responsibility. The particular way in which this is done is relatively unimportant.

Such a conception of the sacramental meaning of birth

is, of course, far removed from the notion that physical baptism is a necessity for salvation. A God who would withhold eternal bliss from a child because his parents or others had failed to sprinkle water on him would be more like a devil than God. In any case He would have no resemblance to Jesus Christ, and the ultimate Christian conviction is simply that the God of the whole world is like Jesus. The real sacrament is not that of water; the real sacrament is the union of flesh and spirit which, by God's providence, makes a new person. It is there already and our task is to make adequate recognition of it. The glory is not that of any human ceremonial act, but rather of God's own creative act.

It is important to note that birth, like marriage, has an essentially public significance. The community has a stake in the child, for he is a potential burden as well as a potential source of strength. The community will educate him and will later profit by his services, as it will lose by his failures or his crimes. From the beginning he is really a member of the group, though it will be long before he can know that this is the case. It is wholly proper that some public recognition of this fact of membership should be made.

The proper mood, as we contemplate childhood, is wonder, but it is not sentimentality. Each child has great and unknown potentiality and each child has a tenderness which constitutes a standing criticism of the older people's hardness, but we are not honest unless we also face the fact that childhood includes a great deal of cruelty. Children are not saints, but frequently exhibit horrible selfishness. The cruelty which school children will show in teasing the unfortunate child or the new child is something which always shocks adults who have not often witnessed it. It is part of the merit of most of the Christian prayer books that they recognize all this fully. The sentimental or romantic conception that children are always lovely and that man, uncorrupted by society, is innately good, may get some support from the naturalistic contemporaries of Rousseau, but it receives no support from Christian theology or from manuals of Christian devotion. The Bible teaches us to be childlike, it is true, but it also teaches us to put away childish things. The best way to deal with children is by a combination of wonder and realism, facing frankly the evil and facing likewise the possibilities of glory. It is part of the secret of A. A. Milne, in the production of children's poems, that this twofold aspect is always kept in mind. Far from idealizing children he has recognized their self-centeredness, making "James, James, Morrison, Morrison," command his mother never to go down to the end of the town, "if you don't go down with *me*." Children are not angels, any more than men and women are, but the combination they represent is endlessly fascinating. Both evil and good are always close to the surface.

The sacramental way is to see each new life as a challenge and as an opportunity, given by God's grace. Here is a new life, fraught with possibilities; how shall we deal with it? The burden is on the parents, but it is also on others, for parents can never discharge their sacred responsibility alone. Those who are unable to have children of their own can find their right places in the total creative life of the world by doing what they can for the children of others. Many women, with no offspring of their own, have done their part magnificently by the teaching of the children of others through many weary, but highly reward ing years.

What we desire for all children everywhere, both others and our own, is not that their lives shall be easy, but that they shall be productive and fruitful. We desire that they be kept from hunger, from fear and from frustration. We pray that they may grow up with strong bodies and with clear minds, and with the inner controls that we call character.

The chief means to this high end, more efficacious than any other, is the family. There is a true sense in which every family is potentially a *holy family*. A mother, a father and little children conduct together an amazing experiment, often in marked contrast to the ways of the world for, in this tiny community, the harsh individualism of the ordinary struggle for existence is consciously and explicitly renounced. The rule is, "From each according to ability and to each according to need." The father, though he works very hard at exacting labor, often receives less from the family budget than does one of the tiny children, especially when the child is ill. The question of what each has contributed is an irrelevant question when the good things are divided. In war-torn Europe the mother who stands in line for food and who works long hours, often eats less than her caloric share, in order that the children may have more than their share. This is one of the chief reasons why the children of Germany appear in better health than observers expect to find. Their mothers do not.

The revival of the sense of the individual family as a

holy experiment would do wonders in our present perplexed and perplexing culture. The great problems seem so nearly insoluble that the individual often feels helpless. We want to *lift*, but we cannot find a convenient or usable handle. Those in ordinary civil life feel helpless because the government does not do more, but those in government, even at the top, feel helpless too. Frequently their hands are tied by prior commitments and by pressures which they are unable to resist. Much of our economic activity is similarly baffling, for the system seems to be larger and tougher than the men who have made it. Steinbeck, in one of his novels, has expressed this sense of frustration by making one of his characters say, "The bank is something else than men. It happens that every man in a bank hates what the bank does, and yet the bank does it. The bank is something more than men, I tell you. It's the monster. Men made it, but they can't control it."

All who feel this sense of helplessness in the face of the magnitude of the modern world can derive hope from the possibilities of any modest family. Here *is* a handle by which we can lift. A family is a unit of such manageable size that we can do in it what we cannot do elsewhere. Within the family there is not perfect harmony, but there is a constantly accepted ideal. In the individual home it is possible to establish our own standards, determine the nature of the major influences and make a separated area of co-operation in the midst of the world's competitive struggle. Each home, imperfect though it may be, is our closest approximation to the Kingdom of God. The ultimate human ideal is a Family of Love. We never succeed wholly in what we try to do in our families, but at least we have a *chance*, which is something we seldom have in connection with larger and more complex human institutions. Within the family we can count on a high degree of true affection and of desire to make the experiment succeed.

When we understand that the home is our best chance to produce a place where love is supreme and where the Kingdom of God can start, we also begin to see that the religion of the home may be more important than that of the church. The Bible speaks of "the church that is in thy house" and most prayer books include services for the home. In this regard the Jewish faith has contributed marvelously to our entire culture, as anyone will realize if he has ever known a devout Jewish family. The ceremony of lighting the Sabbath evening light is something of great beauty. It seems that a good many Jewish homes, now quite separated from the life of the synagogue, keep up various home celebrations, which help their children to resist the secularizing forces of our age. What is so helpful is that the children should come to think of themselves, often by unconscious influences, as members of a family which has standards which are held to be precious, whatever the world outside may do or fail to do.

This sense of belonging, of conscious membership in a family tradition is immensely powerful as a moral force. It is much stronger than anything produced by overt commands. If a little boy in the Brown family begins to feel that Browns just don't stoop to some kinds of activity, he is already deeply surrounded by moral influences. The power of expectancy can hardly be overemphasized. Children tend, on the whole, to do what it is expected that they will do. Perhaps the one influence which a boy finds hardest to resist is that which comes when he is told to "Be a man." What he is *potentially*, begins to determine what he is actually.

We can be helped at this point by the memoirs of good men and women who know something of what their formative influences have been. Thus we can learn much from Dr. Albert Schweitzer in his *Memoirs of Childhood and Youth*, who tells us what started him on the road to equatorial Africa. We owe a special debt of gratitude to that dean of contemporary autobiographers, Rufus M. Jones, who has told us of his childhood influences in three books, *A Boy's Religion from Memory*, *Finding the Trail of Life*, and *A Small Town Boy*. We learn how much he owed to "Aunt Peace" and to all the others in the home in Maine, eighty years ago. On the occasion of his eightieth birthday this universal Christian said:

> I am most of all thankful for my birthplace and early nurture in the warm atmosphere of a spiritually-minded home, with a manifest touch of saintliness in it; thankful indeed that from the cradle I was saturated with the Bible and immersed in an environment of religion of experience and reality. It was a peculiar grace that I was born into that great inheritance of spiritual wisdom and faith, accumulated through generations of devotion and sacrificial love. I never can be grateful enough for what was done for me by my progenitors before I came on the scene. They produced the spiritual atmosphere of my youth. I became heir of a vast invisible inheritance, more important in my life than ancestral lands or chests full of the gold of Ophir. There is nothing I would exchange for that.

These are nobly serious words and should help all parents, who read or hear them, to see more fully the nature of the work which they are privileged to perform in the care of their children. Our danger is that we should be concerned exclusively with the financial inheritance and forget the more important heritage of which Rufus Jones speaks. It is, of course, not negligible to be able to provide our children with good food and adequate housing, as well as schooling, but we may provide all these and yet fail miserably in our central responsibility, which is that of mediating the inheritance of wisdom and faith. If each generation were forced to start afresh we should always be in savagery, because what we call civilization is a cumulative product. There is a true sense in which each generation stands on the shoulders of all generations which have preceded it. Parents are the chief link with this invisible past, without which the life of any child is meager and poor. The central task of fathers and mothers who have been given the sacred charge of new human beings, with potentialities for good and ill, is that of providing the spiritual atmosphere in which young human beings will grow best. Homes are intended to be places of creative transmission of influence.

We can learn a great deal about the glory of family solidarity from other cultures, but especially from the Japanese. The ordinary Japanese family, including those of Japanese ancestry who have been in America for two or three generations, looks upon itself as a unit in which all members have unlimited liability for all others. As against the unrestrained individualism which we sometimes encourage, the Japanese practice is for the children to keep constantly in mind the needs of the entire family, frequently working for years to support younger brothers and sisters or aged parents. It was touching, at the time of the forced movement of Japanese-Americans from the

Pacific Coast, to read the reasons given by young Nisei for desiring to go to college. "Since my family are now cared for by the government," wrote one on his blank, "I am free to go forward with my education." "I want to look after my parents when the war is over," wrote a girl. "They won't be able to obtain work, but if my education is completed I am sure I can obtain the work that will support them."

If we can give something of this same motivation to our children we are doing them a distinct service. Many of them are endangered by the tendency to suppose that they have privileges and rights without responsibilities. If a family can be looked upon from the beginning as a fellowship, in which each is trying to do his part to make the whole enterprise succeed, moral training is already far advanced. We must do what we can to overcome the belief that a self-centered and pampered existence is a satisfactory kind of existence. The notion that children are the best insurance for old age is beneficial both to parents and children, but it is especially good for children.

It is the misfortune of many young people, especially when they first leave home or go to college, to feel that they must revolt against the faith and manner of life of their parents. Sometimes this is mere self-assertiveness, an unlovely phase to be endured as measles and mumps are endured, but there are other situations in which the revolt is unhappily justified. That is always tragic for all concerned, even when some good results arise out of the experience. It should be the aim of all parents to bring up their children in such an atmosphere that adolescent revolt will never be justified. This is not easily accomplished, but there are some striking examples of success. For example, Donald Hankey, telling of his youthful circumstances and teaching, was able to say, "I never learnt to connect religion with narrowness, or with smug self-satisfaction, or with harsh judgments of others, because these features were wholly absent from the religion of my home." It is words like these that every concerned parent would love to hear. To know this in advance is to understand our purpose and to work more intelligently toward an end. All know it dimly, but it needs to be brought vividly into consciousness and held there.

When we seek to envisage the birth and growth of children in the framework of reverence, understanding parenthood as a holy task and not merely as a biological function, we must deal, sooner or later, with the problem of size of family. For many this is a bitter subject. On the one hand there are thousands of couples who are eager to have children, but are unable to do so. On the other hand are the far more numerous couples for whom the danger of too many children is one which fills their hearts with fear. More children will, they believe, make an already difficult economic situation impossible or may ruin the mother's health. The couples for whom the size of the family is no problem clearly constitute a minority. Many couples, with one child, are deeply disappointed because they cannot have more.

There seems to be very little that can be done, at this stage, about the childless marriages. That the problem will not yield easily to medical knowledge is shown by the fact that such childlessness often appears in the homes of physicians. They, like other professional workers and intellectuals, seem to exhibit a greater tendency to sterility than do those engaged in more manual labor. It is now known, contrary to earlier belief, that sterility is almost as common in men as in women. This serious problem cannot easily be solved by the practice of adoption, for the reason that there are not enough children available for this purpose. A doctor in a small town reports that he could place a hundred children at once, if only they were available. The best students of this subject of childlessness do not know why the problem is so prevalent at a certain level of society, though several have ideas that may prove to be correct. It is probable, for instance, that the whole subject is closely tied up with the average age at which marriage occurs. Those who marry early seem to have more likelihood of offspring.

For the most part such studies involve little comfort for those who now live in childless homes, whatever they may mean for future matings. Somehow those who are now without children must find a way of making their peace with the situation, and this is never easy, particularly for the woman. This is where religious faith comes into the picture in a wholly practical way. Religious faith can turn what might have been bitterness into true peace of mind. It is the alternative to frustration, when we come against situations which are beyond human power to change. The devout person prays, "O God, help me to change the evil which *can* be changed; help me to bear the evil which cannot be changed; and help me to know the one from the other." Many who sincerely and devoutly pray such a prayer begin to realize that the world does not stand or fall by the satisfaction of their private desires. If they cannot bear children, they can do something else. There are so many burdens to lift! How wonderful it would be if childless women, instead of trying to overcome boredom in an endless round of bridge parties and club meetings, should seek out overworked young mothers and volunteer physical help. They could stay with the babies for entire afternoons and let the young mothers go out with a real sense of freedom and without the necessity of payment. This sort of thing occurred frequently in the simpler society of an earlier day, but with us now it is almost unknown. It would, however, be a potent solution to the spiritual problem of many childless women.

Where there are a few who have no children, or only one or two, there are millions who live in almost constant fear of pregnancy. What can we say about this problem if we try to place the whole fact of birth in the sacramental frame? The first thing to say is that, in some way or other, there must be a limitation on births. This limitation is required, not by any failure to value human life, but rather by a deep sense of its worth. *It is a wicked thing to bring so many new persons into existence that the lives of all of them are sordid.*

Though birth control is morally defensible, it must never be supposed that this touches the heart of the matter. Family life is made good, not by any mechanical process, but by the ideals and character which become the dominant factors in it. Any practice which purports to eliminate the need of these is an evil practice. Birth control is vicious if it becomes an excuse for unrestrained license without a sense of responsibility. Furthermore it ought to be employed sparingly. It is the judgment of some eminent physicians that the steady use of contraceptives in early married life produces sterility, so that the couple find they cannot have children when finally they decide that the time for a family has come. All this means that there is no easy solution of the problem, that it calls for constant tenderness and control, and that an effort must be made to know the will of God. The act of helping to produce new human beings is so sacred an act, in the light of the infinite worth of each human soul, that it cannot be properly approached except in the mood of reverence. Even then, there will still be problems, but they will be mitigated.

Once there are children, the major task is that of making a really good home or of making a good home better. Central to this is the practice of some kind of family worship. This is admittedly difficult in the modern world, especially when the father and the children leave home at different hours, but it is not likely that the problem has ever, even in an agricultural society, been easily solved. Though in most homes in which family worship has been abandoned, the abandonment has been because of the practical difficulties, there are some who have given it up because it has seemed unprofitable. It is easy to become sentimental about our grandfather's home, with a long chapter from the Bible every morning, but there must have been many homes in which this was little more than a burdensome form. In that case it ought to be given up, but it is our responsibility to put something better in its place. We need the help of one another in trying to find what that better way is.

There is one practice which any family can maintain and which seems to be essential in a home which is undertaken in the sacramental mood, and that is the practice of a time of worship at each family meal. Nearly all families are together for at least one meal a day and, in any case, should sacrifice much else to make this possible. *The table is really the family altar!* Here those of all ages come together and help to sustain both their physical and their spiritual existence. If a sacrament is "an actual conveyance of spiritual meaning and power by a material process," as we have said in Chapter I, then a family meal can be a sacrament. It entwines the material and the spiritual in a remarkable way. The food, in and of itself, is purely physical, but it represents both labor and love in its production and it represents human service in its use. Here, at one common table, is the father who has earned, the mother who has prepared or planned, and the children who share, according to need, whatever their antecedent participation may have been. It is ideal communism in practice.

When we realize how deeply a meal together can be a spiritual and regenerating experience, we can understand something of why our Lord, when He broke bread with His little company toward the end of their earthly fellowship, told them, as often as they did it, to remember Him. We, too, seek to be members of His sacred fellowship, and, irrespective of what we do about the Eucharist, there is no reason why each family meal should not take on something of the character of a time of memory and hope.

Beautiful as a common family meal may be, it is not always beautiful and usually will not be unless a conscious reminder of our purpose is provided. Some meals turn into unhappy occasions of scolding and fierce argument, and each such meal is a tragic failure. There is no foolproof way to avoid this, but long experience shows that the beginning of the meal with an unhurried time of reverent waiting before God increases mightily the chance of success in the holy experiment which each meal is. Those who sit down to food, without a time of such reverence, are denying themselves and their families a potent instrument of meaning.

If grace before meat is to mean what it ought to mean, it must be neither hurried nor perfunctory. Often the members of the family come to the table almost breathless, the children from play and the parents from labor. The temptation is to hurry everything and to get on with the job, but this temptation must be consciously resisted. The prayer rattled off like a formula is almost worse than nothing. Above all there must be a note of reality, and if the children sense that grace before meat is a mere convention, the enterprise has already failed.

Deadness in this matter is best avoided by deliberate variety. Several books should be handy in the dining room, including the Bible, the *Book of Common Prayer* and various prayer books or collections of family devotions. Some families find it helpful to use prayers of different faiths such as those found in the *Hebrew Prayer Book* and the Roman Catholic *Missal.* In reading the Bible, care must be taken to select passages which are full of meaning and which do not sound merely antiquarian or legalistic. Among the best readings are individual parables and individual psalms. Sometimes the family will be helped by a wholly silent grace, with all heads bowed in reverence; sometimes it is good for all to hold hands around the circle, thus symbolizing the unbroken fellowship, while a prayer is said in unison or one of the children prays alone.

Those who lament the decline of the family altar and who are sure that its revival is necessary if we are to recover lost ground, may feel that this emphasis on worship at the common table is not sufficient; they think there ought to be separate times. Perhaps there ought to be, but if the minimum described above were faithfully attempted we should have something so much better than what we now normally have, that there would be reason for rejoicing. This program has the merit that it appeals to many families as something *practically realizable* and not some impossible dream. We are wise if we concentrate on this modest but attainable good, rather than upon an idealized best, which only discourages so many struggling yet well-intentioned and much burdened parents.

In addition to grace at table any normal family can, with a little imagination, make religion seem a perfectly normal part of home life by glorifying the great occasions in the family. The death of a grandparent can become the occasion of a solemn time of quiet prayer for the entire family circle, perhaps about the fireplace. The birth of a new baby can be a time marked by thanksgiving on the part of parents and older children. Even birthdays and other anniversaries can become times of peculiar openness to the sense of God's love and presence. Thus, by degrees, the entire family life comes to be set in the one frame which is adequate to it. Religion, then, is not one single factor in family existence, but is the mood by which a host of common deeds come to have meaning. It is in this way that the precious unconscious influences are preserved.

Our religion is one which challenges the ordinary human standards by holding that the ideal of life is the spirit of a little child. We tend to glorify adulthood and wisdom and worldly prudence, but the Gospel reverses all this. The Gospel says that the inescapable condition of entrance into the divine fellowship is that we turn and become as a little child. As against our natural judgment we must become tender and full of wonder and unspoiled by the hard skepticism on which we so often pride ourselves. But when we really look into the heart of a child, willful as he may be, we are often ashamed. God has sent children into the world, not only to replenish it, but to serve as sacred reminders of something ineffably precious which we are always in danger of losing. The sacrament of childhood is thus a continuing revelation.

CHAPTER IV

Work

The great use of life is to spend it for something that will outlast it.

WILLIAM JAMES

THE most common and the most damaging reaction to the shattering events of our time has been the emergence of an *interim mentality*. Emotionally we are a people waiting for a catastrophe. The bomb *seemed* to fall on two Japanese cities, but in a far more profound sense, it fell on *us*. The sense of temporary living is not always recognized in consciousness, but is with us as the unconscious assumption, underlying all that we do and all that we think. The uprootedness, which was already a mark of our contemporary culture, has thus been vastly accentuated.

The interim mentality by which we now live is bound to destroy us if it continues long, because the good life does not come that way. It is our fate to live at a time when all thoughtful people realize that extinction, both for them and others, is a live possibility, but we dare not stop at this point. What is important, practically, is our reaction to this tremendous fact. The most beneficent form which this reaction can take is the decision to organize our lives *as though* they are to go on, and thus make the fundamental wager. We shall build best if, while we are fully aware of the danger which surrounds us, we proceed on the hypothesis that organized life will continue and that we are building for the generations.

We know, of course, that this policy is a gambler's choice, but there is good reason for gambling in this particular way. The difficulty of any alternative view is that it is inevitably self-defeating. If we react to the crisis of our time by turning away from marriage and disciplined work and other essentials of a permanent society, we are thereby adding to the mood of crisis which can so easily become the mood of futility. As Thucydides long ago suggested, fatalism tends to produce what it dreads, for men do not oppose that which they consider inevitable.

One of the most striking evidences of the mood of futility which has settled down on the Western world is the hesitation of a number of young people to go forward with specialized or professional training. What is the use, some say, of starting upon a long course in medicine or law, only to be pulled out of it in a few years for military duty? Why not live for the moment and at least have a good time while we wait for the inevitable catastrophe? Thus fatalism, as always, is destructive of serious effort.

In many parts of the world the old notion of choosing freely a life work, preparing for it, and then giving an entire life to it, now seems little more than a nostalgic dream. It sounds good, but is unrealistic, they say. How, it is asked, can you plan a life when your major decisions are already being made for you, both by circumstances and by governments? In America, where we have a free economy with all its dangers, we can still choose, except in wartime, what work we undertake, but there are other Western countries, including Great Britain, in which this possibility is not so clear. The British youth considers the live possibility that he may be forced to accommodate himself to a situation in which his life work is determined, not by his own choice, but by the direction of the government.

Though we really cannot blame young people for the sense of futility which settles upon them in these circumstances, the futility is nevertheless an evil. It will only make matters worse. When people cease to believe in the dignity of *work*, discouragement has reached a very low point, a lower point than we have usually known. Many, in the past, have continued to believe in work after they ceased to believe in God or in human love or in survival after death. For a generation, in our universities and colleges, the one sure way of catching the attention of students has been to discuss with them the question of their life work. Nearly every young man has felt keenly the importance of the decision according to which he employs his major powers for the next forty or fifty years. Even those who have claimed that they are not religious have frequently shown a concern about professional life which has included a religious quality. Though they have not normally used the word, they have sought to *dedicate* their lives. They have sensed the need of the world and they have hoped to make their lives count in meeting some of this need.

Professional pride and voluntary subscription to ethical

standards within the professions have been among the most hopeful features of our entire culture. Men have taken pride in being good doctors, good engineers, good journalists. It has been encouraging to see the manner in which young people, while still in the professional schools, begin to identify themselves with their chosen work and let this be the formative influence in their lives. Even when there has been no conscious loyalty to Christian ideals, this professionalism has kept the life of many from becoming decadent. When we try to see what there is that we can start from in the reconstruction of our age, we realize that there is a starting point in the fact that some men still pride themselves on careful shipbuilding and other men pride themselves on accurate accounting.

It is all this, however, which appears to be changing. We may say that the dominant vocational interest was the rule up to about the time of the end of World War II, but that now we are in great danger of losing it. What will happen to a society from which this support is removed is hard to say, but the very danger helps us to see what our task is. We must find a way, even in the midst of our perplexed and perplexing generation, to keep and recover the sense of the sacredness of the work of our hands and brain. What we need is the persuasive declaration that the glory of work is something bigger than our little time and that our task as individuals is to keep the basic idea in circulation. We must teach this generation that the right way of life involves a deliberate choice of life work, *whatever events may do to our plans*. We are not responsible for all world events and we cannot foresee them, but we *can* live by abiding principles in a confused world in so far as our part of the undertaking may go. It is worth while for me to start my medical course whether war comes or not, partly because every added example of stability is a real contribution to our kind of world. The determining events may be beyond our powers, but we can, in any case, make our own decisions and try to carry them out to the very edge of possibility. If enough men and women were to do this the events, themselves, might be different and the completion of intended courses might be possible. In any case we must keep before this generation the enduringly valid idea, so that it may be available when men become sane again.

For centuries Christians have made much of ordination, in the sense of explicit entrance upon the duties of the Christian ministry. Some have spoken of entrance into holy orders as a sacrament and some have not, but all have seen the step as both solemn and sacred. Ordination has appealed to the imagination because it stands so obviously for complete dedication of life and all its powers. Consequently, much has been made, particularly in evangelical circles, of the "call" to the ministry. Men have waited to see whether they have a distinct "vocation," that is, a striking sense that it is the will of God for them to employ all the remainder of their lives in the spread of the Gospel and the cure of souls. Frequently this sense of a call has been ennobling and inspiring to the entire worshiping community in which it has occurred. When, in a revival meeting, some young person commits himself to "full-time Christian service" this is felt by all to be a very high experience. This is especially true when the call involves a sharp break in manner of life. The American public, as a whole, recently had an opportunity to understand this when the famous "Doctor I.Q." of the radio gave up his lucrative employment, studied at Seabury-Western Theological Seminary, and later settled down to the formation and nurture of a rural parish in Texas. Instinctively we recognize the nobility of such a decision and honor the sense of call which made it possible.

Though we have been wholly justified in glorifying this sense of a divine call to the ministry, we have been foolish to limit the idea to such work. If ours is God's world, any true work for the improvement of man's life is a sacred task and should be undertaken with this aspect in mind. We sometimes suggest this by our frequent use of the word "vocation," but we have used the word so long that we have forgotten the degree to which it is a specifically Christian word. If we can recover the original meaning of vocation we shall be doing something important for our present world.

We have made much of the phrase "full-time Christian service," thereby referring to the priesthood, the ministry and to definite missionary work. The supposition is that people are called to these as they are not called to other occupations. Our rule in this matter must be, "not less but more." Instead of full-time Christian service, we shall do well to speak of "full-life Christian service." The really crucial decision comes, not when a person decides to be a foreign missionary rather than a farmer; the really crucial decision comes when a man decides that he will live his whole life in what the late Thomas Kelly called "Holy Obedience." Whether that leads to farming or banking or evangelistic work in Africa is then wholly secondary.

The major decision has already been made and the decision is that to allow one's entire life to be a channel of divine love. This, whatever our work may be, involves a break with a merely secular order. If we were to take our religion seriously we should see the ordination to the priesthood as a sacrament; but we should likewise see ordination to any worth-while human task as a sacrament. It is just as important for one boy to decide to be a Christian business-man as it is for another boy to decide to become a Christian clergyman. If we mark the latter step with special ceremonies of recognition, why should we not mark the former in a similar way? The most damaging criticism which thoughtful young people make of so much current religion is not that it is *untrue*, but that it is *irrelevant*. It is so tangential to life that whether it is true or not makes no real difference. But if our religion is united with the major steps of life, that is, the decisive ones, it ceases to seem either abstract or irrelevant. *No religion is irrelevant if it helps people to see the hidden glory of the common things they do.*

The glorification of vocation is already recognized, in the case of most girls, by the sacrament of marriage and again by that of birth, which we have considered in the two preceding chapters. The Church has been following a deep wisdom when it has made ordination correlative with matrimony. The priest marries the Church as the bride marries the husband, each step being both deeply devout and essentially irrevocable. Both steps are professional, since motherhood is woman's profession *par excellence*. Only a minority of women have any other profession or, when they understand its glory, need any other during their major period of creativity. What we now propose is that, for those women who undertake some other profession than motherhood and for those men who undertake some other profession than the clerical one, there should be a consciousness of the equally religious character of the step which is so crucial, involving so much for so many years of a normal life in normal times.

A Church which seeks to lift our sagging civilization will preach *the principle of vocation* in season and out of season. The message is that the world is one, secular and sacred, and that the chief way to serve the Lord is in our daily work. The missionary task is not merely that of India and Africa, but that of America and Europe as well. The conversion of the world will not come by the efforts of clergymen merely, but by the efforts of all who are deeply committed. Thus there can be one central vocation, while there are many professions. Some persons can contribute most to the conversion of the world by working in banks, and some can do most by working in hospitals. We need guilds of devout politicians, guilds of devout lawyers, guilds of devout scholars. Part of our trouble is that we have so often left the religious job to those who are supposed to be professionally religious. "It's their responsibility, isn't it?" But decline comes this way. The task is far too large for any one group, no matter how deeply dedicated and able they may be. The idea of being professionally religious is really a pernicious idea, anyway, because of the degree to which it seems to excuse the rank and file of a solemn sense of responsibility. Nobody can have my religion for me any more than he can have my health for me. It is wholly proper that some men should give themselves to the professional task of preaching or of counseling, but it is pernicious to suppose they are thereby in more sacred callings than others or that the responsibility of others is thereby lessened.

We have the beginnings of the enlargement of the sense of Christian vocation in some associations of our time. All know of the Gideon Society, made up of Christian commercial travelers who are devoted to the task of providing Bibles for hotel rooms all over the land. Several cities now have associations of Christian businessmen and recently we have seen the formation of a society of Christian professors. These scholarly men teach widely different subjects, most of them supposedly secular, but they look upon their teaching function as a sacred calling. In Washington a little group of legislators now meet regularly for prayer, because they look upon their work of law-making as a holy calling. This movement is small, and seems to have little chance in a city where the normal basis of meeting is not prayer, but rather the cocktail party, yet it is a step in the direction in which we must turn if our common life is to escape ultimate decay.

The concept of vocation changes radically and crucially the way in which a young person approaches his life work or preparation for it. Apart from this concept his major questions often have to do with probable income, personal advancement, manner of living and choice of location. There is no doubt that many now choose their work with these specific considerations uppermost in their minds, for this is the "natural" way. However, one who chooses in the light of vocation has a wholly different standard. His central interest is not in money or professional advancement, but in how he can make the best strokes to help clean up the mess of the world before it is too late. His motto is, "Work while it is day, for the night cometh when no man can work."

The young person who has caught the vision implicit in the idea of vocation looks out at the world and tries to see how its need can be matched by his own latent powers. This, as millions know, is the way in which Albert Schweitzer determined to study medicine after he had already proved himself successful in another profession. The man who lives by the principle of vocation has substituted *concern* for *advancement.* Once he has determined the general line of work in which he will engage, and for which he must train himself by disciplined care, he still has the choice of *where* he will serve, or at least he has this choice in a free or relatively free economy. Will the young doctor practice in the city or in the village? Will he practice in Alsace or in Africa? The person who seeks to order his life by the principle of vocation will study this question very carefully, because in most cases, one decision precludes others. He will answer, in the end, on the basis of comparative need and on the basis of probability of success in meeting that need.

If there is a situation of need and yet no real chance of doing anything permanently valuable toward meeting the need, whereas some other area of need holds out the probability of relative effectiveness, the person guiding his life by the principle of vocation will choose the latter. There is neither wisdom nor piety in hitting our heads endlessly against a stone wall. If they will not listen in one town, Jesus told the Seventy, go to another. Look around, therefore to see whether there is some real chance of accomplishing your aim before you decide to use the little powers you have. Don't play when the cards are known to be stacked against you. Are you convinced that the big bank is so organized that, even if you were to spend your entire life in it, you could never crack what seems to you an inhuman system? Then go to a small town bank where, in time, you may be friend and counselor to the people who need you. Are you convinced that a Christian university is an impossibility in our age because the forces in it are so diverse, divisive and unmanageable? Very well, then, find a small college where there *is* some chance of success, in the major Christian enterprise, even though you know that there the path will not be easy nor victory absolutely assured. It is better to do the little that we can do than to wear ourselves out in frustrated efforts which have no conceivable chance of effectiveness.

It is important to say clearly at this point that the way of vocation is the *only* way for a concerned Christian. A decision concerning life work that is not made on the basis of calling is not a Christian decision at all. Of course, what we usually have, in practice, is a combination of factors. Even the boy who is most deeply convinced of the truth of what is being said in this chapter usually brings in some worldly considerations into his decision, and the self-styled pagan, though he would reject the idea of service as sticky sentimentality, usually reveals at some juncture the desire to make his little life count for something more than his own private gain. His real motivation is frequently superior to his theology or his lack of theology. A consideration which gives ground for hope is the degree to which something of the vocational ideal has permeated our thinking even when we have not been explicit about it. Many young people still feel that they must justify their major decisions by some reference to the good of mankind, so that even the boy who goes into business is comforted by the thought that he can make money and help support those enterprises in which others perform more direct human service.

There are some who suppose that the notion of vocation, when expressly avowed by a young person, is not only unrealistic, in the light of the confused world situation, but a bit pious or even self-important. A man must be taking himself very seriously, it is said, if he considers so carefully the way in which he can do the most good before death or old age overtake him. But the answer is clear! If this sounds pious, let it. The alternative is a wretched world, of which we are getting a clear foretaste now. A boy who tries to decide his future in a sense of holy obedience *is* taking himself seriously, but that is exactly what he *ought* to do. "A man who won't bet on himself," said Will Rogers, "ain't worth a damn." But the young person who seeks a vocation, and not merely a profession, is doing more than bet on himself; he is gambling on the fundamental nature of the world. He is betting that this is really God's world, in spite of appearances to the contrary, and he is trying to find a way in which he can be God's partner. This is not to say that he values his own contribution overmuch, but quite the contrary. He knows how feeble his powers are and how little he can accomplish, but that makes him all the more eager to make his contribution in a manner that will provide some real lift to humankind. If I have only a little to give I am particularly desirous of giving it in the right way and to the right causes. If I were rich I would not need to be careful, but I am not rich. I, therefore, want my little to count.

The ultimate tragedy is the tragedy of waste. It is terrible to waste food when people are hungry, and it is terrible to waste cloth when people are cold, but it is more terrible to waste a life when so much needs doing. It is a common characteristic of all the high moments that one choice inevitably eliminates others. Loyal devotion to one mate precludes loyal devotion to a rival; the spending of money on perfume precludes the spending of the *same money* to aid the needy and suffering; the dedication to motherhood makes impossible an equal dedication to some other pursuits. *Man must choose*; that is his very life. This is conspicuously true in the matter of life work where the almost universal experience is for the groove to become so deep that the individual never leaves it. The years are precious and they are gone all too soon. We must face the fact that every positive decision is also a negative decision; when we choose our work we are voluntarily eliminating from our experience many lines of endeavor in which we might have been successful. The probability is that a man who succeeds in one field would have been able to succeed in several others, providing he had given his mind equally to any one of them, and some men do several things at once, but most men will not.

Though the principle of vocation teaches men to choose their work on the basis of concern rather than upon that of the personal happiness of the worker, the normal result of such choice is happiness in a high degree. There are many unhappy and frustrated people in the world, but not many of them are persons who have found ways of productive work. Not finding joy in the particular work they are doing, they rush frantically to places of entertainment or turn to alcohol. Their "pleasures" are thus an accurate index to their fundamental sadness, largely because they have not found ways in which their tasks can be part of some larger scheme which gives their little lives both dignity and meaning.

Happiness, as Aristotle long ago taught, comes chiefly by some productive act, a working in the way of excellence. Our happiest moments are not those in which we ask how to be happy, but rather those in which we so lose ourselves in some creative task, which seems to us important, that we forget to take our own emotional pulse. When we plant trees, write books, build houses or make roads, we often find that we have been having a wonderfully good time and that we are not immediately driven to do something to have "fun." We have had, all along, something better than anything which commercialized and self-conscious entertainment can ever provide.

Creative production ought to be within the realm of possibility for every human being and probably is, if we learn to seek it intelligently. Very few people can compose symphonic music or paint pictures worth hanging, but these are not the only ways in which the creative urge can express itself. It has been wisely suggested that almost anyone can "build a rustic bench where people for years to come can sit and watch the sun go down."[1] Most of us know persons in humble circumstances who have found

[1] Professor Carl Welty, in an unpublished chapel address at Beloit College.

remarkable peace and fullness of life by modest productivity. One of the most enviable men I have ever seen was an old man in North Carolina with a sorghum mill. He had a wonderful pride in taking the juice of cane stalks and turning it into sorghum almost as clear as honey. He had found a chance to *create*, in the production of excellent sorghum. Consequently, he was both an artist and a man.

The tragedy of so many millions in our modern age is that they have lost most of the sense of the dignity of the day's work. They have no sense of its dignity because the principle of division of labor has been carried to such a degree that it is extremely hard for each individual to feel that his small part has any meaning in the whole. Of all the evil things that industrialism has done to the human race, this is one of the worst. It is relatively easy for the humble stonecutter on the cathedral tower to feel the nobility of his work, as he sees the tower rise slowly day by day, but it is not so easy for the worker in the automobile plant to feel the same sense of participation in a creative act. He knows, of course, that cars are rolling off the far end of the production line, but what he daily sees is only one segment of the gigantic shop. Losing the reward of joy in work, he, like the owners, struggles for more financial rewards, and thus gives a push to inflation, *because his only real satisfactions come from the spending of money*. There are some fortunate people in the modern world who are so situated that their work is their pleasure. When they are away, on holiday, they can hardly wait until they get back to the job. Their occupation is their hobby and they are well-organized people. Unfortunately, these fortunate ones now seem to be a minority, because millions hate what they are doing and find their major pleasures outside their work.

Most of us feel extremely helpless when we contemplate a problem of this size. We are very sure that industrialism has come to stay and that the clock cannot be turned backward. We know that most boys in the modern world do not decide between medicine, law, journalism, ministry and agriculture, as ways of making their finest contributions while they are able, but decide instead *which factory* to enter when they get out of high school. Perhaps, therefore, what we are saying belongs to an unreal world after all. But it must not. We do not know the answers, but to know the problem is something. Reinhold Niebuhr spoke for many in our time when he said recently, "There was a time when I had all the answers. My real growth began when I discovered that the questions to which I had the answers were not the important questions."

Of this we can be certain, that if we do not find some better solution of the problem raised by the sense of meaninglessness, which so many in our time have in connection with their daily work, we cannot long maintain our culture or even our high standard of material living. People who have no sense of the glory of their work, people from whom has departed the whole idea of work as sacramental, will not long do good work. Our civilization will then cease to advance and a civilization which ceases to advance is already, as the late Professor Whitehead taught us, in full decay, because advance and decay are the only choices open to mankind. It is in this connection that we begin to see that the Christian ideology may have far more practical significance than we normally suppose it has. Perhaps it is only by a revival of the sacramental nature of work that even our industrial and economic problems will be solved.

Meantime we can go forward with the program of making as many individuals as possible convinced of the vocational ideal. For some this will necessarily mean a change of work, while for others it will mean new developments in the work now being done, particularly developments on the human side. Recently a man engaged in a well-known distillery sought a complete change, along with preparation for new work. Inquiry revealed a truly heartening motivation. He already had a good income, he was surrounded by friends and he liked his town. Why, then, should he change? "Well," he said, "it's hard to express, but perhaps it is that, at the end of the day, I want to feel that I've pulled my weight." He knew that life is short, that we cannot do very much, but he did not wish to waste the little potentiality that was his. He did not want, at the end, to feel ashamed. He was not willing to come to the end of his threescore years and ten and be forced to admit that he had never done anything except help make a little whisky.

We are tempted to say that all work is equally valuable and therefore equally sacred, but it would be sentimental to say so. Though it is probably true that every job has its good side and includes opportunities to serve mankind, some jobs are far more valuable than others, because of the difference in the character of the final product. There are jobs into which good men would be ashamed and rightly ashamed to enter. Not all professions are open to committed men, because some are essentially predatory or parasitical rather than truly productive of the goods and services which are sorely needed. It is nonsense to say that the man who accepts bets at the race track is in a job potentially as noble as that of the farmer who produces grain and meat. Any work can be improved by having good men in it, but good men must know that some avenues are far more conducive to human service than are others.

A sad human predicament in which many men find themselves is that in which they recognize the area in which their best contributions could be made, but feel constrained, by circumstances, to stay in something else. "I know now what I ought to have done all along," a man in his thirties says, but unfortunately it is too late to change. Such a person usually has unavoidable family responsibilities, a certain standard of living which he supposes he must maintain, and a measure of security which he hesitates to lose. But the man who stays in the secure path, never making the break in the direction of his real interest or sense of calling, will become an increasingly unhappy and frustrated man. The way of wisdom is to make the break and to make it at once in spite of difficulties and temporary or permanent sacrifice. The sense of using one's only life rightly is so important that real sacrifice, even on the part of the rest of the family, is wholly justified.

A variant of this way of living is found in those careers in which different important things are done at different times, with a clear break at each step. This is to live one's life in chapters; it may be all the same book, but with different chapters in it. Thus a man may engage in business, but be unwilling to give his entire life to business pursuits. He may plan, early in his career, that, if he has sufficient means to do so by the time he is fifty, he will break his active business connections and devote the remainder of his days to unremunerated public service. This has actually been the accepted practice in a few circles and has been a beneficent influence in their communities. Not only does this provide communities with expert service of undoubted integrity, at no expense, but it also does wonders for the "retired" man. Instead of using his declining years in dashing from one resort hotel to another, in a vain and ridiculous effort to bring back vanished youth and its pleasures, such a man finds new avenues and new joys which are utterly different from those of his earlier business experience. The same plan of life will hold good in various professions and not merely in business. After all, it is rather dull to go on making more money just to leave it to the government or for others to spend. Far more wonderful would be the experience of using the precious and hard-won economic freedom for some service of permanent worth that might not otherwise be accomplished.

The strongest reason for living life in chapters is that there is so much that is possible and it seems a shame to miss every part except one. Wouldn't you hate to die without having drunk of the cup of life more deeply? A good illustration of how life in chapters may produce, not a scattered life, but a rich one, is provided by the career of the late Lord Tweedsmuir. This remarkable man, John Buchan, was for a while a scholar, for a while a civil servant, for a while a professional writer, for a while a soldier, and finally Governor-General of Canada. He died, not remarkably old, but full of days; he had lived richly though not expensively. His autobiography, *Pilgrim's Way*, is a constant inspiration to many readers, including the writer of this book. Not all can do it as well as John Buchan did, but something of his way may be adopted more widely than we realize. It may, for instance, be adopted by vast numbers of women. The noblest career for a woman is motherhood, but the chief features of this vocation come rather sharply to an end when the last child leaves home. What then? At this point many women lose interest in life or try to "entertain" themselves by going about. But, if they were wise, they would see this as a glorious opportunity to use freedom for new pursuits. This is the chance to take up painting, or Hebrew, or classical archaeology or a thousand other things. Life is never long enough to allow for more than a fraction of such vastly interesting and spiritually rewarding pursuits. How foolish to waste any of the hard-won freedom by pining for what is irrevocably gone or turning frantically to a round of supposed amusement! Life is altogether too short for such stupidity and waste.

Though life in chapters can be thrilling, not all people *ought* to live their lives in this way. Physicians, for example, are so sorely needed by ailing humanity that it would usually be wrong for a man who has acquired skill in healing to turn to other things at the age of fifty, no matter how rewarding those other things are. What is the path of richness for such a person? This path lies in having more than one side *all along*. Even without the clean break of retirement, the physician can give an increasing amount of his time to other interests, leaving some of his professional work to associates. Thus Ray Lyman Wilbur, while always a physician, has been able to be university president, cabinet member, writer and director of philanthropic agencies. Usually Dr. Wilbur has been able to do several of these at once and thus make his experience rich all along. In a similar manner Jan Smuts has had more than one side to his interesting life and has usually been able to be both statesman and philosopher at the same time. It is hard to say whether he will be remembered longer as the veteran prime minister of the Union of South Africa or as the author of the distinguished Gifford Lectures, *Holism and Evolution.* He has been able to keep both sides of his life together, now stressing one and now the other. Most human beings could have a modicum of this richness if only they would take their little lives with sufficient seriousness.

When we think about it deeply, we realize that what we desire and what we require is some achievement, no matter how modest, which makes a difference. We should hate to come to the end of our days only to find that we had merely gone through the motions, carrying the bricks up the hill and then carrying them down again. Life is unbearable unless it has meaning, and the chief way in which it can have meaning is for our little effort to contribute to some larger whole. The work of the mason is glorified if it helps to build the cathedral; the sweeping of the hotel room is glorified if it helps to recreate the lives of the persons occupying that room so that they, in turn, can do better work toward some high goal. The ultimate goal is the conversion of the world to the spirit of Christ, which would then demonstrate a really loving fellowship, the one reality which all agree would be a terminal and not merely an instrumental value. The problem is to see how, given our particular powers, we can contribute most to such an end.

Some of the finest contributions to this end come from those whose work seems to be of a humble nature. The work of the Pullman porters is a case in point. It is unlikely that these wonderful men, who seem to be paragons of patience, have any idea that they are making valuable contributions, but that is exactly what they are doing. Many of the people they serve are, in turn, enabled to serve more productively. A Negro woman who has cooked in the home of a prominent American writer for more than forty years ought to be able to feel that she has had a part in the literary product, for it would not have been possible, at the same efficient level, without her aid.

It is part of this requirement of meaning in existence that the contributions we make should be permanent or at least not wholly transitory. We have a deep desire to make a difference, not merely today, but tomorrow as well. This is one of the ways in which eternity is set in our hearts in an inescapable fashion. Motherhood, by this standard, becomes the most satisfying of vocations because every common act, from washing faces to teaching the multiplication table, is intended to have future and not merely present effects. It is hoped by the mother that cleanliness may finally become habitual and that the product of common integers may be known by second nature.

The most vivid way in which we demonstrate our flair for the eternal is by our effort to do work that lasts. "The work of our hands, establish thou it" (Psalm 90:17) we cry in every generation. To live merely for the moment, conjugating endlessly the verb "to eat" is not really to live, at least not on the specifically human level. To live on the human level is to try to write a poem which will enrich the experience of persons still unborn, to build a garden wall that will grow in beauty with the years, to produce a law that will help to ensure future justice; these are ways in which men and women can find significance in common life. People who find such paths do not normally blow out their own brains or turn to that escape which we call alcoholism.

It is reasonable for man to desire a monument, because he is always resisting his finitude, but his true monument is not something in a cemetery; it is what he has produced, be it farm or machine or painting. It is heartening to know that the best monuments are often erected in the most disturbed and perplexing times, times like our own. Many have been helped, in this connection by the inscription found in the chapel at Stanton Harold, near the heart of England, which tells of a man who sought in the days of the Cromwellian turmoil, to do something lasting. The inscription reads:

IN THE YEAR 1653
WHEN ALL THINGS SACRED WERE
THROUGHOUT THE NATION
EITHER DEMOLISHED OR PROFANED
SIR ROBERT SHIRLEY BARONET
FOUNDED THIS CHURCH:
WHOSE SINGULAR PRAISE IT IS
TO HAVE DONE THE BEST THINGS
IN THE WORST TIMES
AND
HOPED THEM IN THE MOST CALAMITOUS.

In our modern world millions find it very hard to know how to dignify their lives. Most of them cannot build a church or do anything else on a grand scale. Most of them must work in factories and shops and, when war comes, they must enter the armed forces. They feel like bees in the hive, rather than free moral agents who exercise voluntary choice in determining the nature of their permanent contributions to mankind. We cannot change all this in a moment, but the best way to begin to change it is to recover a largely lost sense that work *ought* to be sacred. It will help us mightily and make us less patient with the present situation; it will cause us to struggle together to find a way. We shall achieve some of this divine impatience over the mechanization of man if we hold before our minds the constant conviction that the common work we do is a share in the creation which is still unfinished, and that *work*, along with *marriage*, *birth* and *death*, is a window through which the divine light can shine in a peculiar way.

CHAPTER V

Death

Be sure that God
Ne'er deigns to waste the strength He deigns impart!
ROBERT BROWNING

THE major experiences of common life reveal what is in men as fire reveals what is in crude ore. They reveal pitilessly either our poverty of spirit or our resources. We know a great deal about a man by the way he reacts to a marriage or to the birth of a child. For sensitive men these are experiences of wonder, conducive to reverence, but for others they are mere secular occasions. Frequently a bit of the hidden life tries to break out, but the fear of seeming pious or sentimental or ridiculous, drives the hidden life back to its hiding place. Sometimes the crucial experiences cause individuals great surprise in that they have suddenly revealed to themselves depths of which they were not formerly aware.

Of all the sobering and revealing experiences, death is paramount. It has become the noblest theme of poetry and of narrative or dramatic writing. Beautiful as love poetry may be, the poetry which faces the fact of death is superior to it. There would seem to be two reasons for the superiority of death over all other human themes. The first of these is that death is a greater leap in the dark than any other; we go to a bourne from which no traveler returns; we know and can know very little of what is on the other side of this chasm which we cross. The second reason for the superiority of death as a moving human theme is its universality. This universality constitutes a marked difference between death and the other supremely revealing experiences of human life in that it is genuinely universal, while the others are nearly so. Not all persons fall in love and marry, not all achieve parenthood, and not all find satisfactory creative work, but every son of earth knows that he will die and, what is more to the point, he knows that his beloved will die. He looks at his child and he knows how little it would take to destroy this happiness. A germ in a drop of water might be sufficient.

It is not the recognition of a man's own death which moves him most deeply, but rather his consideration of the death of others. When our time comes, we may be entirely unconscious of our own demise, since many die in sleep, but we are highly conscious of the death of those whom we love and also of millions of others such as those who die in wartime. Though we become partially hardened to the experience of mortality it is always deeply moving to the sensitive person and we never quite make our peace with it.

That the death of another may be far more revealing than is the contemplation of one's own end is shown by the perennial discussion of the problem of evil as well as the chief arguments for immortality. It was not the prospect of his own death, but the retrospect of the death of Socrates that seems to have driven Plato to believe that this life could not end all. In a rational world it was impossible to suppose that a life of such nobility and fairness could be brought to a complete end, merely by the injustice of a few Athenian judges or by the administration of a bit of poison. In the series of arguments presented in the *Phaedo*, Plato is wrestling with the problem which the death of Socrates presents, not chiefly the problem which his own death will bring. The ordinary good and thoughtful man does not begin, as some critics have supposed, by believing in immortality for himself because he, personally, desires it; he begins rather by noting the manifest injustice involved in the death of someone else and drawing the necessary conclusion from the postulate that this is, in the end, a just world. Since justice is not done to some in this life, there must be another life succeeding it; otherwise the very demand for justice is finally frustrated. But very few men, when they sincerely present this argument to their minds, are thinking of their own injustices or their own eternal deserts. It is more common for a man to recognize that he may have nothing in his own life worth saving, so that his hope rests, not on his own merits, but on divine grace. It is not shocking to me to think of my own life coming to a complete end, but it is shocking to think of the life of my beloved as coming to such an end.

It is desirable that, as honest men and women, we should face squarely this transcendent fact of death. We are not living wisely or well unless we recognize that whatever we prize most we hold by a slender thread which may, at any moment, be broken. Though it is possible to face this in such a way that our present lives are glorified and our future tragedies made more endurable, the sad fact is that many try to escape the inevitable event and consequently face it suddenly without preparation. Anyone who has ever seen proud and fortunate people suddenly crushed knows how serious this situation can be. The usual supposition is, "It can't happen to us." *But then it does happen,* and then we find that we are woefully unprepared. Yet we could have been prepared, at least in part, and we could have done this without any morbid preoccupation with the tragic such as might dim the ordinary beneficent joy in human living.

There is some accumulated wisdom on this subject, inasmuch as so many of the poets and prophets of our race have given their best thought to it; and their fundamental agreement is very striking. On the question of one's own death the agreement is especially marked, partly because this part of the problem is simplest and easiest to solve. The wisdom of centuries, put magnificently by Robert Browning in "Epilogue to Asolando" is: *Make all the strokes you can while you are here and leave the event in the hand of God.* We do not need to worry about how justice will be done to us, because that is not our responsibility. Our responsibility is to work while it is yet day and trust that, if the night comes, God is the Lord of the night as truly as of the day. The ultimate wisdom lies in being able to say,

> I only know I cannot drift,
> Beyond His love and care.

But Browning and Whittier are only echoing the wisdom of the Psalmist, "The Lord is my light and my salvation;

whom shall I fear? The Lord is the strength of my life; of whom shall I be afraid?" (Psalm 27:1). The British poet, the American poet and the Hebrew poet belong to the same company and it is a goodly company. We are not likely in our day, in spite of our technological advance, to learn anything more profound than what these poets have already said.

The important thing is not merely to know what wise men have said, but really to *feel* it. The combination of work in the present and trust in God's grace for the future must become a settled habit of mind. It will help us to recognize that there are limits to knowledge. Then we can pray humbly with Johnson,

> And while it shall please Thee to continue me in this world where much is to be done and little to be known, teach me by Thy Holy Spirit to withdraw my mind from unprofitable and dangerous enquiries, from difficulties vainly curious, and doubts impossible to be solved. Let me rejoice in the light which thou hast imparted, let me serve Thee with active zeal, and humble confidence, and wait with patient expectation for the time in which the soul which Thou receivest, shall be satisfied with knowledge.

There may be persons who look upon such a prayer from the pen of the literary giant of another age as mere pious writing, but there are others, and they are among the most sensitive men, who find in them the very water of life. Suffice it to say, that any person who can, with intellectual honesty, pray such a prayer and *mean* it, has already reached the place where the problem of his own death has ceased to be a problem. He has learned how to live and he has also learned how to die.

The harder problem arises when we try to counsel others

who have lost what they prize most in the world or when we face such loss in our own experience. Is there any wisdom about this? The experience of mankind is that the sorrow cannot be *eliminated*, but it can be *glorified*. This is done chiefly in two ways:

(1) We can put the experience in words which express it nobly and place it in a frame which dignifies it. This is a religious service. For thousands of years men and women have felt that an act of worship was the only suitable way of *celebrating* death, and to this end they have turned quite naturally to certain noble passages of the Bible which say incomparably well what ordinary men would like to say and cannot.

It is far better when the expression is restrained; it is wise to say something less than we feel, rather than more. The older type of funeral, which emphasized unrestrained emotion, was almost wholly bad, and bad because it permitted self-gratification. There is no escaping the fact that much of our human grief is purely self-centered and that our tears are often tears of self-pity. The glory of the great Biblical expressions is that they maintain the mood of objectivity. We are sorry, not for ourselves, and not for the one who is gone, but for the loss to mankind, as we move into the great theme of the world tragedy as a whole.

The elevated quality of the latter half of the fifteenth chapter of First Corinthians, a passage central to so many funeral services, is truly miraculous. The noble words give us exactly what we require. We want our little sorrow lifted up and glorified by participation in a universal experience that takes us to the very heart of God and the meaning of reality. I am carried beyond my own little sorrow and into the life of every man when I can say or hear: "So also is the resurrection of the dead. It is sown in corruption; it is raised in incorruption: it is sown in dishonor; it is raised in glory: it is sown in weakness; it is raised in power: it is sown a natural body; it is raised a spiritual body." How would it have seemed to be present while the inspired tent maker of Tarsus was dictating these deathless words and signing his name with his own hand?

What we cannot bear, in the midst of tragic separation, is triviality. Sorrow is bearable, men find, not by denying it and not by minimizing but rather by rising to the level of tragedy. The most moving of all tragedies, the crucifixion, is shot through with sorrow, but when we see it as a revelation *of* men as well as a revelation *to* men, we cannot call it evil. What I should find very hard to bear would be to have the death of my beloved marked by some merely sentimental or inferior expression, but I could bear the loss, I think, if it were given an adequately noble expression. I should writhe under the sentimental song, but I should be wonderfully strengthened if I could hear some devout person say, with real meaning:

> For this corruptible must put on incorruption, and this mortal must put on immortality. So when this corruptible shall have put on incorruption, and this mortal shall have put on immortality, then shall be brought to pass the saying that is written, Death is swallowed up in victory. O death, where is thy sting? O grave, where is thy victory? . . . But thanks be to God, which giveth us the victory through our Lord Jesus Christ. Therefore, my beloved, be ye steadfast, unmoveable, always abounding in the work of the Lord.

We are tempted to avoid the subject of the loss which a bereaved person has sustained, but this is almost always a wrong policy. People who have suffered loss usually desire to talk about it and they *need* to talk about it. The man whose beautiful and gracious wife has died is eager to talk about her with those who have known and loved her too. His own high estimate of her character is corroborated by each person who relates some experience with her. This reminder of what he has lost helps him to be thankful for what he had so long and of the past joy which no event can ever take away from him. Instead of pining over present loss he becomes increasingly grateful for past joys. The lover likes to hear of his beloved, whether living or dead, and the fact that this accentuates his sense of loss does no harm. *He desires to feel his sense of loss and not to have it minimized.* Men are not hurt by sorrow as much as they are by frustration. The people to pity are those who are so shut up in their grief that they cannot find any expression of it, whether in the Christian context or any other.

Here is where the trusted pastor, especially one known for years, is such a boon. There are some good arguments for short pastorates, but they have no bearing on the problem of death in the community. Nearly everyone, when he comes to life's deepest moments, craves the help and counsel of one known for years. We may be glad to play golf with the relative stranger, but we should like to have an old and trusted friend sit with us when the house grows suddenly quiet and we are alone. The chief dividends in the Christian ministry come when a pastor has lived in a community for many years, shared the joys of his people and helped them to adjust themselves to a multitude of circumstances. The person who walks with us to the open grave should be more than the occupant of a priestly office; he should be a *friend.*

(2) The other major way in which sorrow can be glorified, though not eliminated, is by the whole-hearted acceptance of a faith big enough to give even the deepest sorrow its proper place. What is required, and what we covet for needy men, is not faith in any particular detail of what the afterlife may be, but simply *faith in God.* Any other faith is always a corollary to it, and without it the rest is groundless. The ultimate expressions of such faith are to be found in Psalm 23, Psalm 139 and John 14. The simplest and perhaps the most profound words in the world are, "The Lord is my shepherd, I shall not want," and "In my Father's house are many mansions," which is more accurately and meaningfully translated, "There are many rooms in my Father's house." The faith, herein expressed, is the faith that all the world is one house, and that, if we move out of the present room of our finite existence, we are not thereby going out from under the loving care of the Father's roof, but only into another and perhaps a more wonderful room.

Though we crave this faith for ourselves and for all men it is now denied most men. The result is pathetic. The characteristic modern man faces the world without shield or buckler, for he does not know the noble passages mentioned above, he is not really acquainted with any secular poetry, he has no real connection with any church. He has never heard the Christian faith, or any other, presented seriously as intellectually valid and he consequently supposes, in his ignorance, that it cannot be so presented. He is uprooted culturally and disinherited spiritually. But death is no respecter of persons and it comes to these impoverished and vulnerable people as it comes to others.

In their pathetic lack of faith the characteristic men and women of our day grope. The cocktail bar which seemed to be sufficient before tragedy struck, is seen as no resource at all, and many have no other. The only outlet for emotion which some know is the pagan funeral with the nauseating expense of flowers and bronze casket, as well as cement vault, all topped soon by the ostentatious stone monument. But such costly display is a poor substitute for a living faith and is deeply unsatisfying.

There is no simple solution to this problem of faith, because there is no substitute for the real thing. What we must do is convert a whole generation to a faith which we cannot say has been lost, because it has never been seriously held. Anyone who has any wide experience of the climate of opinion of our time knows that the modern mind is shot through with ethical relativism so that millions do not even believe in an objective moral order. Morals, it is widely believed, are the products of societies and one man's meat is another man's poison. The natural result is that confusion is truly appalling.

The great Horace Bushnell once preached a sermon in the Yale College Chapel called "On the Dissolving of Doubts." He told how, as a student in the divinity school, his faith in God practically ceased, but when he almost touched bottom there was one fact which he found one could neither doubt nor deny: that there is an eternal distinction between right and wrong. Starting from this base, Bushnell built up his faith again, but the marked difference between his age and ours is that the very fact which he found indubitable is one which the vast majority of modern men and women do not believe is a fact at all. Consequently they have *no* place to start and they flounder helplessly.

It is part of the good fortune of our time that we are now in possession of some of the most brilliant intellectual defenses of the central faith that mankind has ever known. Contemporary theology is marked by a galaxy of great names, such as it would be hard to match in other generations. Thanks to these giant minds there *are* answers to the doubts and perplexities of modern man and constant floundering is not necessary, but the mistake is that the convincing and persuasive material has not been brought sufficiently to the attention of the average man, who is accordingly out of date in his thinking or lack of thinking. This is why far more preachers should have the courage to preach on the central themes of theology, presenting their evidence fearlessly and unapologetically in the language which the modern man understands. We must begin at the center. What the bereaved man needs is not the comfort of some platitudes about death; what he needs is a living faith in the Living God, and then he can comfort himself.

If people, by the honest use of their intellectual powers, come to believe in God and if they, then, open their hearts in such a way that they come to know Him at first hand, overcoming the ordinary barriers to such awareness, the rest is relatively easy. Then everything will be seen as having potential religious significance and the lost provinces of Christian faith will return to their homeland.

It is perfectly clear that death is largely a lost province. In countless modern communities the place where the bodies of the dead now lie has no relationship to the place where the living now worship God and nobody seems to consider this strange. Most burials and cremations occur in cemeteries which are ornate, pagan, commercial establishments, and a very large proportion of the funerals are held in "undertaking parlors." A prominent clergyman, recently called to a small town to conduct a funeral, protested because the service was not held in the church, only to be told that there had not been a church funeral in the town for more than ten years. The townspeople had ceased to think of death as falling within the orbit of the church; it belonged instead to a commercial interest. They expected, it is true, to have a clergyman or a lodge conduct some kind of funeral service, but the real center of operations had moved to the establishment of the mortician. This is the fault, not of the mortician, but of the responsible churchmen.

There is hardly any feature of our culture which exhibits so vividly, as does this, the alteration that has taken place in the pattern of American living. It was not always as it is now. When America was settled the conception of the church still dominant was that of the "meeting house." The place of worship was at the geographical center of the community and constituted likewise its architectural focus. Frequently the church was the scene of political meetings, as well as occasions of a purely religious character, and sometimes, in pioneer days, it was the scene of secular learning. In those rare communities in which the ancient pattern is unbroken, the cemetery adjoins the church and sometimes practically surrounds it. It is as natural, in such a setting, to bury one's dead in the churchyard as it is to mail one's letters at the post office, because the church is understood as the organ of *the entire spiritual life.*

One of the great advantages of the ancient institution of "God's acre" is the consequent effect upon generations of worshipers. We lose something very important when we are forced to worship weekly in a building which has about it little or no hint of the existence of former generations. Such an experience is a surface affair; it leaves out the dimension that gives depth. If, on the other hand, we can walk to church across ground dotted with simple stones intended to perpetuate the memory of neighbors of many generations, we are fortunate, indeed. Then we can, the more easily, have a sense of the human story as an ongoing enterprise. Then we can understand more vividly something of what it means to share, ever so humbly, in the communion of saints. Then we can enter the church and sing, with peculiar significance, "O God, Our Help in Ages Past."

The church has, for a generation, been beating a steady retreat, giving up positions which have been promptly occupied by commercial interests. The latter now have a virtual monopoly in regard to burial, and they are gaining ground in regard to the funeral itself. Many undertakers have built rooms having a semi-ecclesiastical appearance and frequently these "chapels" have staffs. The undertaker finds it profitable to employ, either part time or full time, both an organist and a clergyman. Sometimes the great commercial cemetery, with a chapel of its own, hires its own clergyman. Thus a completely secular institution, with a financial stake in death, and in the sorrow which accompanies it, makes some pretense of admitting the relevance of religion, but we are gullible indeed if we suppose that this constitutes a continuation of the ancient Christian pattern or that vigorous religion comes this way. It is true that the undertaker often introduces a bit of pseudo-Gothic into the construction of his funeral chapel, but such a room is by no means a church, for the important reason that it is not a meeting house. The church is the right place to make some suitable and humble recognition of the mystery of death, because it is likewise a place of life. The church is a place where *all* the greatest mysteries are celebrated and where each part gains by participation in the total scheme. Why are funeral parlors inevitably depressing, whereas most older parish churches are not depressing, even when bodies are buried under the pavement? It is because the funeral parlor has abstracted one experience out of its context, whereas a real church resounds with the happy songs of little children, the immemorial declarations of faith, the prayers of thanksgiving, and the glorification of human love.

Just as the undertaker's chapel is by no means a church, however much it is made to look like one, so the cemetery chaplain is by no means a genuine minister. He is a paid servant of a corporation and it is not a religious corporation. He is not a shepherd who knows and loves his flock, to whom men and women turn for help because they have had reason to trust him long before. The cemetery chaplain is a functionary and, in the nature of the case, can be nothing more. He may be an impressive reader of a ritual, but he has practically no opportunity to know the people whom he supposedly serves, just as the justice of the peace often has little opportunity of knowing the people whom he legally joins in marriage. Though it is tragic that so many of our fellow citizens now have no real church connection, there may be a tiny forlorn hope in the fact that so many are yet sufficiently wistful to turn to wretched substitutes and pay for them.

All who read these lines will be well aware of the almost insuperable difficulties which prevent a recovery of the ancient pattern. In modern cities, with the price of land so great, it is frequently impossible for a Christian community to afford to own burial ground, and many churches have no unoccupied space around them at all. Even the fine old city cemeteries, such as those about the older churches of Boston and Philadelphia, have, for the most part, not been used for actual burial for many years. Moreover, some residential communities have ordinances prohibiting burial in populated districts, even though the churchyards have ample room, such ordinances having been inaugurated, in many instances, under the pressure of those with a financial stake in their inauguration.

In view of such difficulties, one must admit that it is hard to know how to reassert the work of the church in connection with death, but somehow we must find a way. Meanwhile, we can at least condemn the current backwardness in taking advantage of the opportunities we still have. Many new churches are built in surburban or sparsely settled communities, where there are neither legal nor financial barriers, and yet the place of burial about the church is not a part of the picture. Many city people could make use of country churches far more than they do, since hundreds of them have unused and uncommercialized space around them.

Rather than purchase land for burial, at fantastic prices, thus enriching the persons for whom the cemetery is nothing but a business venture, many concerned Christians are today turning to cremation as a practical solution of the problem. Even then, however, the expense is often great, partly because of the fact that embalming is demanded by law, and caskets are required, even when both body and casket are to be burned in a few moments. Thus our modern laws make almost impossible the simple, inexpensive handling of death which might be reasonably expected if we were to take our religion seriously. We make so little headway in the direction of simplicity because each family faces the issue singly and is ashamed to seem niggardly or even economical in the presence of an experience so overwhelming.

The best wisdom in this matter is for families to make a deliberate effort to envisage the problem in advance, making some sort of plan, so that decisions of such importance will not have to be made under the stress of great emotion. If the members of the family know all along that they do not believe in expensive and ornate caskets, if they know what kind of service they would find helpful, and if they know what disposal they propose to make of the body, a sudden crisis can be met with a certain degree of calm. Since death is inevitable this cannot be interpreted as borrowing trouble or being unnecessarily morbid. Whether we decide to bury or to cremate is relatively unimportant; what is important is that our decision be made in a cool hour, so that it will not be regretted later. It must not be supposed that there is any one particular way which all should follow, though there are certain principles which ought to be observed. Different families will come to different decisions on details and this is as it should be.

Though burial in the churchyard is difficult today, a funeral in the church is easy to arrange and not expensive. The only hindrance here is the fact that, for the most part, the church has not been sufficiently bold in its expectations. People tend to do the expected thing, and it is part of the task of church leadership to set the tone of the community. It seems likely that most people do not deliberately choose the more secularized funeral, but accept it simply because the Christian alternative has not been made part of their normal expectations. Most decisions, in the midst of sorrow, are made quickly and without sufficient counsel. All too often, when death occurs, the family calls the undertaker first and, if the minister is called at all, he arrives *after* the primary decisions are made. It is not presumptuous of Christian ministers to suggest to their congregations a reversal of this order.

There would be great gain if, in our cities, villages and rural communities, we should again be able to assume, without discussion, that the church is normally the scene of life's highest and deepest and most searching experiences, whatever they may be. Our culture is largely pagan today, but there are signs, on all sides, that men and women are not permanently satisfied with a life so devoid of meaning. It is our task to challenge the secularization and fragmentation of society by reaffirming a Christian faith which is large enough to include all aspects of human experience, one of the most important of these being death and the proper recognition of it. It is, of course, true that the sorrow of men and women, when they lose those whom they most deeply love, is not assuaged by any words that can be said in a church or anywhere else. But if sorrow cannot be assuaged as we have suggested earlier, it can be dignified. It can be lifted up and placed in a Christian frame. Parents who have lost a beloved child may be as sad as ever when the service is over, but there is great gain in the realization that the religious community has shared the sorrow, that ancient declarations of confidence in God have again been expressed, and that the entire experience has been given the only appropriate setting which men know.

If we were to try to handle death in a really Christian way, how should we do it? Perhaps it would be something like this: As soon as possible after death occurs, and with the least possible expense, the immediate family with some trusted spiritual counselor, would take the body to its place of either burial or cremation, so that what was dust could turn again to dust, either slowly or rapidly as the case might be. Most Christians would feel the necessity, at the graveside or in the crematorium, of a simple statement of faith, such as the twenty-third Psalm, a simple prayer and some reverent silence without the intrusion of any words, even the best. All this could be done without the presence of curious observers. Then, a day or two later, when the public had been given sufficient notice, there could be, in the natural place of worship, a memorial service in which people, by their very presence, could testify to their affection for the one gone as well as to friendship for those remaining. The life of the one taken would be remembered and this memory would be lifted up into the general framework of belief in the love that casts out all fear. The memorial service might, as sometimes actually occurs, become a time of thanksgiving and rejoicing over the friend so long known and loved. One such memorial service was held under a giant oak which had provided daily shade for an invalid woman almost to the time of her death. As her friends and neighbors gathered under the tree, her bereaved husband, whose tenderness toward her had been well known, sat with the company and mingled freely with them at the close. Not a tear was shed, because the memory of the woman's life was so bright and so cheering. In so friendly a gathering it would have seemed queer for any mourners to sit behind a screen. In a sense there were no mourners for all were rejoicers. They were glad for the gift God had given them rather than mournful because it was taken away. And the woman's own faith that underneath are the everlasting arms seemed to pervade the entire company.

There is little need for an expensive display of flowers at such a memorial service, since there is no casket to cover. In view of the fact that so many neighbors wish to make some kind of gesture of respect, some communities are now encouraging particular memorial projects, dear to the heart of the deceased, to which people so desiring can contribute. The potential gifts to worth-while projects under this plan may be considerable, in view of the fact that flower arrangements are extremely expensive. It is not uncommon, in some communities, for the total floral display to add up to a thousand dollars. The practice of substituting books for flowers and placing them in the public library, with suitable memorial plates, is widely diffused in Sweden and is gaining some ground in parts of America. There is no reason why we should omit all flowers, since flowers are very lovely, but the Christian faith, when taken seriously, will oppose the vulgar display now so common.

If the body of the deceased is buried, the problem of a suitable marker soon arises. It is a good thing that we have markers, because it is a rich human experience to wander through an ancient cemetery and try to think of the lives memorialized there. The perennial nature of this appeal is sufficiently proven by the fact that Gray's *Elegy Written in a Country Churchyard* is the best-loved poem in our language. There is, therefore, no rational or Christian objection to the erection of headstones, but there is very great objection to the modern tendency in the direction of ostentation and display in this matter. One does not have to be very well schooled in human life to note that frequently the largest stones are erected to the memory of the worst scoundrels. Here, more than in most cases, the first rule is simplicity and the second rule is simplicity, also. If we do not appreciate this already we can learn to do so by noting the contrast between an ordinary burial ground, with its stones competing in grandeur, and a Moravian cemetery, where all the stones lie flat on the ground and all are alike, symbolizing the deep equality of brotherhood in death. Americans who travel in England frequently manage to visit the beautiful country meeting house in Buckinghamshire, called Jordans, where William Penn and his family are buried. The famous colonist's last resting place is marked by a stone not over fifteen inches high, standing near the doorway of the beautiful seventeenth century meeting house where he worshiped as a young man. Those who see the simple beauty of such a scene can hardly help being in revolt against the display which we have so often taken for granted.

It is a good thing for men to face the fact that they will die. We exhibit our power, we parade our learning, and we display our wealth, but these seem to mean remarkably little after a short time. We are now having our little day as millions of our predecessors have had theirs, but within a hundred years we shall be gone from the scene and very few of us will be remembered by anyone. Man may learn, in his ingenuity, to postpone death a bit and to ease its pains, but he cannot overcome it. Death is the great democrat who, in the end, levels all our pretentions. We cannot, therefore, do anything about death, but that is not our province. We can, for a little while, do something about life. We can use our powers to help arrange some little area in such a way that they shall sit every man under his own vine and under his own fig tree; and none shall make them afraid.

Life, though brief, can be glorious. There are some who have lived it magnificently as they have tried to think God's thoughts after Him and to be to the Eternal Goodness what a man's own hand is to a man. Such people have been deeply devout, but their religion has not been something apart from basic human events like loving and dying. Their religion has been the way in which common experiences like loving and dying have been glorified by being placed in the framework of divine grace. This is our great tradition and it is such a pattern which we must now restore.

The Willson Lectures

SOUTHWESTERN UNIVERSITY

1948